THE TEMPLARS
(BEYOND A MYTH
OF THE MIDDLE AGES)

THE TEMPLARS
(BEYOND A MYTH
OF THE MIDDLE AGES)

EMMANUEL BARCELÓ

© EDIMAT BOOKS Ltd. London
is an affiliate of Edimat Libros S.A.
C/ Primavera, 35 Pol. Ind. El Malvar
Arganda del Rey - 28500 (Madrid) Spain
E-mail: edimat@edimat.es

Title: *The Templars*
Author: *Emmanuel Barceló*

ISBN: 84-9794-030-X
Legal Deposit: M-48228-2004

PRINTED IN SPAIN

INTRODUCTION

There are few Great Enigmas of Humanity as exciting and complex as that of the Templars. They were children of the Dark Middle Ages, when knights had taken over from the Greek and Roman heroes, uniting in their Order the dual condition of monks and knights. This gave them licence to raise their swords against infidels, never before permitted at the heart of the Church.

The Church had only previously been accustomed to martyrdom as the sole defence of its faith, and suddenly it found itself the owner of great property and territory and as such required to defend it. Within Europe, kings and Christian noblemen already performed this task on its behalf; particularly Spaniards, through a Reconquest against the Moors that was centuries old. In Palestine, however, the Church had lots of territory but no-one to defend it. Moreover, that was the Holy Land, the centre and origin of its faith. Was it acceptable for infidels to control this land?

Thus it was that Hugues de Payns' opportune offer along with his eight brothers-in-arms to create a religious military order was considered worthy of authorisation by papal decree. They came with good references from the king of Jerusalem in addition to knowing the pilgrim routes like the back of their hands and the best way to protect them from continual Saracen assault.

But this Order was to find itself far from European influences, living among Muslims who worshipped Allah and his

5

prophet Mohammed and whose customs, social life and religion were very different from those of Christ's followers. They survived there for nearly two hundred years, during the midst of extremely cruel wars, moments of peace and such close cohabitation that on occasion they were equal almost like brothers. In addition to all this, the Templars succeeded in discovering the secrets of the Kabbalah, opening Salomon's mysterious chests, learning about ancient texts that granted immortality to a scarce few, through elixirs, long periods of self-sacrifice and control over human weaknesses.

Since all the knights that joined the Temple were educated, they had a great sense of value and curiosity and they soon realised that power was obtained from great wealth. That was the reason why they created the first banks, owned their own fleet of ships and helped in the construction of the great Gothic cathedrals. They received many large donations, both from the Holy Land and the different countries they settled in; nevertheless, it is possible that at least a few of them managed to obtain the philosopher's stone, the alchemists' great dream that would enable them to turn any metal into gold.

The annihilation that none of them were able to effectively contain presents us with another mystery: were they perhaps not afraid of death because they were convinced of their own reincarnation?

We are certain that you will ask yourself many questions as you read this book, since that is our intention. We have written it like a great novel, in which all the literary ingredients are included, and yet the facts recounted are true, proven by historical, archaeological and some first-hand testimonies. We shall leave the mysteries in the air, although we believe we have solved some of them while others remain to be solved, in the hope that this will fuel your curiosity. It is possible that, in time, you will manage to solve some of them yourself.

Chapter I

THE BIRTH OF THE ORDER
OF THE TEMPLE

Fear of the Apocalypse

The West reached year 1000 A.D. full of fear. False prophets, dire soothsayers and opportunistic monks had announced the end of the world, the coming of the Apocalypse. The streets teemed with penitents, communities began to fast and the sky was cloaked in the darkness of superstition.

Ploughs were abandoned, men and women left their houses, traded in their normal attire for black habits and fell into line behind the saviour of the day. Never had so many prayers been said, nor such wrenching laments been heard. Many covered their hair in ashes, publicly proclaiming their sins.

However, so deep were the ranks of the repentant that no-one listened to their fellow man with a critical or accusatory ear, but rather as a means of exposing their own weaknesses. One might say that people were plagued by guilt and, thus, willing to subject themselves to the harshest penance.

When the self-incriminations abated, the religious men who led the march, brandishing crosses lashed together from branches, shouted out psalms and intoned songs of atonement like an endless march toward crucifixion.

Suddenly, in the midst of this massive, crazed and frenzied penance, came the dawn of 1001. Life had not ended, nor had the dead been 'resurrected.' Some of the penitents continued to roam, driven by fatalistic inertia. The majority went back to their homes, or what was left of them.

Whole families had perished in the penitent wanderings. Others had been decimated. The few that survived intact were forced to adapt themselves to the new circumstances. Some accepted the role of serfs; the more fortunate found ways to restart their lives. But none would ever be the same.

Amazingly, no-one was blamed for the endless calamities. They were accepted as if they had been but the consequence of another epidemic, something inevitable. And they neither reduced the attendance of the faithful at church, nor diminished the immense power of the monasteries.

Europe of the monasteries

Europe had not been Roman for over five centuries. The barbarian raids from the North had turned everything on its head. Cities were pared down to the bare minimum, transformed into castles. Kingdoms abounded, and the fear of invasion was greater than ever. There were hardly any coins, since bartering, the exchange of certain products for others, was preferred.

The institution that knew best how to adapt itself to this enormous revolution was the Church. Through the construction of enormous monasteries, it centralized teachings, trade, libraries and, above all, the relationship between knights and vassals. These monasteries became Medieval Europe's main cultural centres.

One of the very first monasteries was built in Montecassino, where the Benedictines established a closed and self-sufficient community. This they were able to do thanks to their founder, Benedict of Nursia, a hermit who lived from

480 to 537. This wise man managed to attract a large following of disciples.

Inside the monasteries, time was controlled with exacting precision: six hours were devoted to manual labour, almost always related to agriculture; four hours to prayer and meeting collective needs; the same number to teaching and study; and what remained to rest. However, the monks were not solely concerned with their own material or spiritual survival, for one of their first missions was to rescue the past and conserve the present.

Since the villages were embroiled in a constant state of war, the Benedictines saw to the preservation of Greek and Roman sculptures, to copying classical manuscripts and to studying the teachings of history's great thinkers. Laudable work it was indeed.

Soon, more monasteries and abbeys were built, and their numbers increased with the appointment of Benedictine Popes. They understood the importance of these cultural centres, which had, by opening their doors to heirs to the throne and almost all of the sons of nobility, come to be true axes of power.

Papal bulls were issued freeing the monasteries from some of their ecclesiastic obligations, at times going so far as to release certain monks, the most important professors, from their duty to attend daily mass. The monasteries also received all kinds of substantial donations, turning them into small kingdoms ably administered by men of the cloth wielding considerable power.

With the construction of the Monastery of Cluny, a primitive university was founded that would eventually produce Roman art. Years later, the Monastery at Cîteaux would give rise to Gothic art. Moreover, both religious centres, in particular the latter, would fuel the idea of warrior orders. This was made possible because the monastic orders had become the centre of all ecclesiastic political power in the West.

The myth of Knights

Knights first appeared in Christianity at the beginning of the ninth century, and they lasted until the twelfth. Somewhere between fact and fiction, we find Arthur, Lancelot, Tristan, El Cid and many others. Most were great lovers of their ladies, serfs, slaves and the dispossessed. However, their conception of justice was rather peculiar, for they cared more about charity. Above all, each was a hero, a champion.

Since war had become a profession, a habitual way of life even, for society's governing elements, the Europe of the Middle Ages bore witness to chaotic periods of interminable, bitter conflicts between members of the feudal cavalry. The Church tried to put an end to these evils by lending knighthood a certain religious character.

Meanwhile, the calamities entailed in feudal struggles were efficiently mitigated through the invocation of institutions such as peace and the truce of God. Almost simultaneously, the bellicose passion of the knights was channelled toward external endeavours, above all the fight against Islam. This new spirit culminated in the Crusades.

Access to the rank of knight, originally consecrated through ceremonies of Germanic and pagan origin, was now completed with markedly religious symbols. In noble families, the knight's initiation began in childhood. The boy was delivered unto the monarch or a wealthy member of the landed gentry, in whose court he was educated as a page and, later, as a hunting, travelling or war companion for the lord. Thus, he learned to ride, fight and behave like a knight, until, his apprenticeship as a squire over and his military abilities proven, the youth was finally armed.

The ceremony, which had mainly consisted of the handing over of the sword, was gradually complimented by other ritual acts, such as the blessing of the weapons or the purifying bath of the aspirant, who, before he was vested, spent a night in prayer, then received the communion and swore to use his weapons for holy and just causes, the defence of the faith and the protection of the feeble and helpless.

In this way, the order of knighthood was eventually perceived as an extensive spiritual group, uniting all noble Christian warriors. As a result of the first crusade, the so-called military orders were born, made up of knights wholly dedicated, through vows, to furthering the ideals at the root of the ecclesiastic-monastic organisation. In short, the idea of the monasteries came to have a military variant, born of a skilled interpretation of the sacred texts: "The religious man shall never lift his sword against his brother, no matter the damage caused; but, should he ever be threatened by an enemy of the faith or have to defend the Holy Land, the situation would be quite another, for then he would be bound not only to lift his sword but also to give his life for the cause."

The Founder of the Order of the Temple

Hugues de Payns was born in the region that gave him his name. The exact date is unknown, but it was possibly around the year 1080. When we first hear of him, he was already an officer for the house of Champagne. He most likely held an important post, for two documents have been found in the archives of the Count of Troyes bearing the signature of Hugues de Payns.

He is also known to have participated in the first crusade, as a commander in the army of the Count of Blois and Champagne. His displays of bravery, as well as his easy way with words, allowed him to forge a friendship with Godfrey of Bouillon and, later, with Godfrey's two brothers: Baldwin and Eustace of Bologna.

At the same time, he met their cousin, Baldwin du Bourg, Count of Edessa and the future King Baldwin II of Jerusalem. All of these contacts would be vital for the future of Hugues de Payns.

Years later, he returned to the East as a captain for Hugues of Champagne. By then, he was already married, and his son, Theobald, would one day become the abbot of the Cistercian monastery of Sainte-Colombe de Sens.

In 1118, Hugues de Payns and eight knights, 'all eternally God-fearing', went to Baldwin II, who had just been crowned King of Jerusalem, and stood before him without forgetting that years before they had savoured his friendship.

"Your Highness, we have come to offer our services as guardians of the road for the pilgrimage from Jaffa to this holy city where you reign," said the French knight, one knee bowed to the floor. "Allow me to clarify: we have scouted out the terrain with utmost care, we speak the Arabic tongue and we shall not act without your authorization."

"My authorization is yours, my brother," answered the monarch, with no need to look to his advisors. "You have come at a most opportune time, for many are the human lives lost at these crossroads."

The new 'monk-knights' were treated as the best of guests and, the next morning, were given the gift of permanent lodging, located at one end of the palace. It took up the entire temple of Solomon. Days later, the monks who cared for the Holy Sepulchre gave them a terrain located next to what was already theirs.

Since Hugues de Payns and his eight companions were now masters of almost the entire ancient temple of Solomon, they were christened the Knights of the Temple.

In no time at all, they began to defend the roads, and they had no need to unsheathe their blades, for their mere presence sufficed to dissuade all types of attackers. They also enjoyed the support of the Patriarch of Jerusalem, Gormond de Piquigny, before whom they had taken their three vows as monks: poverty, chastity and obedience.

Nevertheless, such submission on the part of strong, healthy, intelligent knights was hardly logical. Any one of them could have met greater fortune crossing the Pyrenees, for all were French, to render their services to any of the myriad kings and counts who had been fighting the Arabs that still occupied more than half of Spain for years. In fact, many had placed their swords and steeds at the service of such causes, and testimonies exist offering proof of the intervention of international mercenaries in the initial years of the Spanish Reconquest.

Thus, we are faced with the first enigma, maintained by some historians, including Louis Charpentier, author of "The Mystery of the Cathedrals": might the Templars not have been in Jerusalem searching for the Ark of the Covenant or the Tablets of the Law? Two religious jewels that offered their possessors immortality and the power to dominate men?

This is not an easy question. Still, many wise rabbis had sworn that these treasures were hidden in the very temple of Solomon... Did the original Templars find them?

Nine years later, Hugues de Payns and five of his companions travelled to France, where they sought the support they needed to found their Order with all of the guarantees. They brought letters of recommendation from Baldwin II, who had financed the journey, and was no longer unknown in the Holy Land.

The Templars served the pilgrims greatly, and in turn they received more and more donations. Word of their ability to win friends among Christians and infidels alike had spread to the four winds. Many were the Sultans and Arab emirs that feared them.

Might they have numbered not nine, as historians insist, but rather many more? Bearing in mind their interventions on the road from Jaffa to Jerusalem, as well as the many occasions on which they successfully came to the aid of the army of Baldwin II, it is impossible to accept that so few Templars were responsible for so much.

The council of Troyes

By 1127, Hugues de Payns had garnered the support of Abbot Bernard of Clairvaux, the future Saint Bernard, who convinced Pope Honorius II to hold the Council of Troyes for the sole purpose of authorizing the founding of the Order of the Temple. Never had the likes of this been seen before.

Two archbishops, ten bishops, seven abbots, two scholastics and a plethora of other church figures attended the Council. It was presided over by the cardinal legate Matthew of Albano, but the voice that rose above them all was that of Abbot Bernard. Almost everyone in attendance was bound to this deft, sage holy man one way or another. As a result, he was able to work things to the utmost advantage of Hugues de Payns.

Of course, de Payns knew just how to use his oratory prowess before this illustrious gathering of theologians and eminent Church figures. He laid out the order's principles and initial services and then adeptly fielded all questions, never ceasing to show the habitual humility of one who makes requests but would never dream of demanding.

The interrogation lasted weeks, and at times it was harsh and incisive, but only superficially, for behind it all Abbot Bernard never ceased to pull the strings. Thus, the Council kept all it considered good about Hugues de Payns' proposals, while correcting those points it found irregular or wanting improvement.

Finally, the Abbot of Clairvaux was charged with drawing up the definitive text, which, in a matter of days, was approved by all in attendance at the Council of Troyes. So the Order of the Temple was 'officially' founded. Its rules were written in Latin, spanned sixty-eight articles and included an introduction that was a kind of exhortation to the Templars' religious duties:

"You who renounce your own wills, you who serve the king with your horses and arms for the salvation of your souls, strive always to hear the matins and the service in its entirety according to canonical law and the orders of the regular masters of the holy city of Jerusalem..."

CHAPTER II

THE ADVANCEMENT
OF THE TEMPLARS

A Significant Advantage

From the beginning, the Templars wished to make it clear that for them their religious duties would always take precedence over their military ones: it was their belief that a Christian comforted by divine favour, having received the communion, would be more inclined to martyrdom. Logically, the goal was not to send the new monk-knights to their death. On the contrary, given that they were such excellent warriors, they were far more likely to triumph in any battle they fought, bolstered by the added aid of God.

In 1139, Pope Innocent II issued the *Omne datum optimun* bull, which afforded the Order of the Temple an important advantage. By virtue of this, the Order was no longer generally dependent on Episcopal jurisdictions for its chaplains and priests; furthermore, it was exempted from paying taxes of any kind. Only the Cistercians had ever been shown such favour before.

This advantage stoked the flames of envy among some of the religious orders, and forever after they would pursue

Hugues de Payes and his monk-knights and all those who followed in their footsteps as Templars.

Abbot Bernard tried to mollify this threat with his work 'De laude novae militiae', in which he sketched the following portrait of the Knight Templar:

"Each one holds discipline to be a devotion, and obedience a form of respect for his superiors. They come and go at the command of he who wields authority. All wear the attire they have been given, and none would nary contemplate seeking food or garments elsewhere. These knights unfailingly adhere to a simple, shared and joyful existence, with neither wife nor child. They are never idle, nor do they engage in frivolous pursuits. They show no signs of considering themselves better than their fellow men. All pay more respect to the brave than the noble. They detest dice and chess, would never partake of the hunt, shave their heads bare, never groom and hardly ever wash. Their beards are eternally bristling and dishevelled. They go through life covered in dust, and their skin is hard and weathered by the heat and their coats of mail.

A Knight of Christ is an eternal crusader, for the fight he has undertaken is twofold: against the temptations of the flesh and blood and, at once, against the spiritual powers of the heavens. He proceeds intrepidly, ever watchful to his right and left, his chest protected by his armour and his soul girded by faith. With this double protection, he fears neither man nor demon. So, go forth, O knights, and drive off the enemy before the Cross of Christ! Know that neither death nor life can separate you from His mercy! Glorious will be your return from the battle and blessed your death, should it occur, as martyrs in combat!"

It should be noted that in this era washing and grooming were seen as signs of weakness. For this reason, when a knight in combat wore his coat of mail for weeks on end it was taken to be a noble feat, despite the scores of lice and other parasites he was forced to endure and the inevitable layers of grime and miscellaneous filth.

Hugues de Payns Entered into Action

The Templars now had rules and a uniform: white habits

and capes for the knights, black for the lower ranks and squires. Later, in 1145, Pope Eugene III would grant them the right to wear a red cross on their right shoulder.

Hugues de Payns left for England, where the dukes of Normandy ruled. He bore some kinship to them and was thus warmly received. They offered him lands and permission to recruit, as well as to accept all types of alms. Better still, they opened the doors for him to all of the churches and let him speak in the squares. As a result, he attracted a sizeable following, both in England and in Scotland. Moreover, he sowed the seeds for future volunteers, who were not able to follow him then due to family obligations. Remember, he spoke to them of defending the Holy Land, the primary focus of concern for all good Christians.

Meanwhile, the Templar Godfrey de Saint-Omer was doing similar work in Flanders. In addition, other Templars had journeyed to Spain and Portugal, where the reception was even warmer, if such a thing were possible, for in these lands a permanent battle was waged against the Arabs. Entire villages, castles, windmills and other properties were placed at the disposition of the Order of the Temple.

Why all the generosity? Had the Templars somehow mysteriously acquired the communicative powers of the very apostles of Jesus? The documents they carried and their words hardly seem to warrant such gifts. Could there have been something more?

This is another of the riddles that accompanied these monk-knights over the course of their brief existence, for their ability to gain riches, exclusively through donations, has yet to be equalled by any other religious order in the world. And we must not forget that they only asked, never obliged. Perhaps, over time, they learned how to make their own gold, through alchemy, which, if true, would plunge us deep into the territory of fathomless mysteries.

The structure of the order

By 1163, the structure of the Templars was firmly established. It was composed of knights, chaplains, sergeants or squires and servants and craftsmen. All obeyed the orders of the Grand Master of the Temple in Jerusalem. However, the Grand Master himself was subject to the vote of the majority, namely, of the Chapter, with regard to his decisions on the most important issues: the appointment of the different province commanders, declarations of war, the signing of truces, laying siege to fortresses and even the induction of new brothers.

Success in Europe meant that Templar commanders had been left in France, England, Flanders, Spain, Portugal and other countries. All were entrusted with administering alms, looking after the brothers under their charge and, above all, sending as much money as possible to the Holy Land. A task they unfailingly executed with overwhelming efficiency.

The choice of the Order's new master in Jerusalem fell to twelve knights and a chaplain. This master had to take up permanent residence in the Temple of Solomon and was to fit the following description:

"He shall always bear a staff and a whip: the former, to fortify weaknesses, the latter to punish signs of cowardliness and mistakes on the part of the brothers."

Strangely, upon closer examination of this master's rights, we find that the rules had undergone a qualitative change. Whereas the nine founding Knights Templars had taken vows of poverty, to the extreme of showing themselves willing to ride two to a horse, their leader now had four mounts to himself, in addition to a special charger for combat. His assistants included an Arab secretary, who doubled as an interpreter, a light cavalry soldier, a blacksmith, a cook and two foot servants.

Is not such an entourage more worthy of a small king than the leader of an order of monk-knights who had vowed never to own any material possessions save for those absolutely necessary to live in times of peace or to fight in times of war? The changes did not stop there.

The Knights Templars now had a seneschal, a marshal and a commander of the kingdom of Jerusalem, who also acted as treasurer. This is but a taste of the considerable hierarchy that marked the Order of the Temple, which also had its own chaplains and priests, each of whom had taken the same vows as the knights. Thus, they were only subjugated to the Grand Master of the Order and the Pope and had no obligation to answer to regional bishops.

Faced with massive numbers of aspiring married men, a special bull was obtained to accept them as mere affiliates, not entitled to share the dwelling of the other Knights Templars. For one of the main recommendations in the Rules of the Temple was this:

"We deem the excessive contemplation of the female visage to put religion at risk; moreover, under no circumstances shall anyone ever dare to lay a kiss upon a woman, whether she be a maiden, widow, mother, sister, aunt or any other form of kin to a member of the Order..."

Of course, such recommendations, like the primary rules themselves, had to be heeded 'as if they had issued from the very mouth of God'.

The ritual of induction into the Order

Hugues de Payns recruited just over three hundred future Knights Templars in Europe; however, many former participants in the first crusade who had stayed on in the Holy Land were also accepted. Since the Temple rules not only allowed for the incorporation of such noblemen and brave knights, but also deemed them essential due to their extensive experience, strong efforts were made to recruit them.

First, however, the future Templar was obliged to resource his lay existence in order to become a monk-knight. Since this process did not, in itself, suffice, the rules were read out, and then a complete exam was conducted before a court of the twelve eldest brothers.

Usually, this took place in the church of the Order, the candles lit to ward off the blackness of night. The candidate would wait in an adjoining chamber, dressed in a white tunic, his head bare and divested of all arms. At a given moment, the two eldest knights would seek him out and ask him these two questions:

"What is your name? What has brought you to us, when you know that in this militia you will be subject to hard work and battles that might well rob you of your life and that, moreover, you will be bound to an existence in which the pleasures of the outside world will not be yours to enjoy?"

If the candidate's answers were convincing, the pair of initial examiners would then return with the other ten knights that made up the Chapter. In ritualistic language, they would narrate all that had taken place. Soon after, the candidate was led into the church.

There, the candidate humbly introduced himself and was offered his first explanations. After hearing his brief responses of approval, a speech such as the following was given:

"Brother, you must not enter the Order wishing to obtain riches or honours, nor out of the belief that you will be lifted to a higher plane or will find yourself surrounded by comforts. Remember, three things will be required of you: first, that you leave behind all worldly sins; second, that you place yourself at the service of Our Lord; and third, that you be the poorest of mortals, eternally subject to penance for the salvation of your soul. Only for these reasons should you request your induction. Are you prepared to become a servant and slave of the Order from this moment forth and for the rest of your days? Are you prepared to renounce your own will forevermore, to obey whatever order your commander might give at any time?"

"Yes, Sir, God willing."

At this point, the candidate was led out of the Church. The master would then step forward, lay his hands over the Gospel and, in a steady voice, address the Chapter with the following words:

"Should any of you know any cause for which this man does not deserve to be our brother, let him speak, for it is better heard now than when the aspirant stands once more in our presence... Shall he return in the name of God?"

"Let him return, in the name of God."

When the candidate was brought once more before the Chapter of the Order, he would publicly renounce his prior life and agree to become a slave of the order. The master would then ask him a range of questions about his military experience, health and social status, whether he had debts or was moved by any other interest. Since the answers were usually acceptable, he would be obliged to take the following vows:

"Brother, listen carefully to what we shall say: Do you swear unto God and Our Lady that, from this moment forth until the end of your days, you shall heed the orders of the Master of the Temple and the commanders that are your superiors? Do you swear unto God and our Lady Saint Mary that you shall remain, wholly and without exception, forever chaste? That you shall have no possessions? That you shall always be in condition to adhere to and respect the good manners and customs of our house? That you are willing to help in the conquest of the Holy Land of Jerusalem, according to your God-given strengths and powers? That you shall never abandon our Order, be it for a strong or weak cause, or a worse or better motive?"

As soon as the candidate's final assent was heard, he was admitted into the Order of the Temple. He was reminded that he was entitled only to bread and water, humble garments, a simple bed, a life of near misery and hard work. Finally, he was given the mantle of the Templars, a cross and a sword. Once he had gathered them up, the master and the chaplain gave him the kiss of fraternity and chanted the hymn used by almost all religious orders:

"How good and beautiful it is to live with your brothers, be one among equals!"

Thus ended the induction ceremony and the candidate became a Knight Templar with all of the same rights and duties as his brethren. Logically, he had to submit himself to a short period of apprenticeship or adaptation to his new life. But he was never alone, for at his side stood the best instructor.

The equipment of the new Knight Templar

The new Knight Templar was wholly responsible for the equipment he received. He was forbidden to give even the humblest of his garments away and was expected to take meticulous care of it all. "For his dress and external appearance were to offer the best portrait of his status as a monk-knight."

As personal attire, he was given two shirts, the same number of undergarments and cloaks (the winter one lined with sheep or calfskin), a fur-lined coat, a hood, a cape, a tunic, a thick leather belt and two caps (one of cotton, the other of felt).

For his bed, he was provided with a straw mattress, two sheets, a lightweight blanket or simple cover and a heavy blanket. All bore black and white stripes to symbolize the colours of the Temple, as well as the Cross, which, needless to say, was always sewn or painted in the most visible spot.

The allotted military equipment included a cuirass or coat of mail to protect the head, leaving the face uncovered, two iron boots, a similarly iron skullcap, a helmet, shoes, a sword, a lance, a triangular shield of metal-cast wood, three types of knives and a horse blanket or mantel to cover his steed.

Before entering into combat, he was also given a stew pot, a bowl for measuring out barley and six saddlebags.

CHAPTER III

THE FIGHTING WAS NOT ONLY IN THE HOLY LAND

The second master of the Templars

It has been written that the master Hugo de Payns died on 24th May 1136. The exact cause of his death is unknown, although one thing we are sure of is that it happened in fighting. He must have 'moved on to the next life' particularly satisfied with his work, for the Templars were thoroughly implanted in society, respected by all, and even if some enemies did remain they were not very powerful ones, and they were also continually were receiving generous donations.

The second master of the Order of the Temple was Roberto de Craon, known as 'el Borgoñés'. He was of noble stock, considered 'a valiant, well-mannered knight, skilful at the bargaining table and possessing an alert mind'.

He formed part of the 'nine monk-knights' who began to act on the way to Jerusalem from Jaffa, before receiving permission and lodgings from Balduino III. What is not quite so certain however, is what drove him to join the Templars. Speculation has pointed towards a failed romance, which some historians doubt given Roberto's elegance, beauty and way with words.

It is certain that if we listen to the legends, in which we are told that the future second master of the Temple planned to seduce a particularly fine dame, inheritor of Chabanis and Confolans, we can then deduce that it was not due to a sentimental disillusion, but rather a question of political interests: Roberto's sweetheart would seem certain to have been betrothed to a nobleman, with the idea being to consolidate or enlarge the property he would inherit. This was a common practice at the time, when even unborn boys and girls were already promised in marriage in order to seal political pacts between counties and kingdoms.

Of interest here is the fact that Roberto was named master of the Order of the Temple after Hugo de Payns' death and followed the path his predecessor had trodden: he obtained papal bulls conceding the highest possible autonomy to the Templars.

The expansion of the Templars in Spain

The first battles waged by the Templars took place in the lands of Spain and Portugal, where for centuries the people had been involved in a long and bloody crusade against the Arabs. International troops also played their part, such as in 1064, when an army made up of troops from several countries set out from Toulouse to recapture Barcelona.

When the Templar Order crossed the Pyrenees, they were expecting to face a full-force open battle, and not the isolated operations against the attacks of bandits on the roads or bands of thieves who ransacked townships. In those times in Spain, King Alfonso I of Aragon and Navarre had already recovered a large part of the Ebro Valley and the city of Saragossa from the Moors.

Right from the first battles, the Templars demonstrated skilful manoeuvring, a clear vision of the objectives and a surprising precision when it came to executing strategies. As they were not restrained by any social binding, their aim was straightforward – to destroy the Muslims in the fastest and most effective way possible. What most stood out in their actions was their military strategy, which they had learned from the Muslims. To the normal custom of the cavalry attacking alone, the Templars introduced the tactic of the infantry. Once the army had formed columns, the foot soldiers started firing arrows to protect the cavalry when it was time for them to lead their attack on horseback. They in turn protected the infantry with their long lances. In this way, the cavalry and the infantry defended and protected each other side by side.

Another well-known tactic employed by the Knights of the Temple of the reconquest of Spain was the *turcoples*, or brother sergeants, who were the scouts, and above all the communication link between the cavalry and the infantry. All this strategy, new to Europeans, had been used by the Muslims, who were able to move more swiftly and lightly due to the fact that they carried little heavy weaponry.

The Spanish and Portuguese monarchs, counts and other nobles of the lands were taken by surprise, despite having fought for so many years against the Moors. This led them to show great generosity toward the Templars, who received many gifts in thanks, such as the castle of Grañena by the Count of Barcelona, constructed on the lands they had recovered for the Spanish. It is interesting to read the document of ceasefire, in which the nobleman was careful to redact the following sentences: "All this I hand over to better defend Christianity, in accordance with the intentions with which the revered Order of the Temple was founded."

Such phrases were used over and over again in other similar documents, such as that signed by Armengol IV, Count Urgel, when he surrendered the castle of Barbara to the Templars Roberto, the Senescal, and Hugo Ricard. The castle was never intended as a gift, rather a type of payment for services rendered, as all these properties had been seized from the Arabs.

The admiration that the Templars earned with their actions was so extensive that Alfonso I created the Order of Montjoy as a way of nationalising the situation for the French Templars. His gesture, however, did not stop the respected foreign troops from being handed the fortress of Calatrava.

25

Even so, Alfonso tried to go further still, for he was coming to the end of his reign (he died in 1134) and had no direct heir to his throne. He wanted to divide his kingdom equally between the Templars, the Hospitallers and the canons of the Holy Sepulchre. All of which was in order to benefit of the religious forces that were defending the Sacred Lands at the time.

The importance of knowing when to renounce an inheritance

However, the Templars refused this generous offer, perhaps because they foresaw the impossibility of administrating such a territory, and also due to the number of enemies that may rise against them. They preferred to wait for the situation to evolve naturally, and moreover, asked for the advice of the master Roberto of Craon.

The master arrived in Spain nine years later, after having waited for the problems that had arisen in the kingdom of Aragon to be resolved. The Templars preferred to keep him at a distance from the events, while they occupied themselves with the reconquest.

In 1143, Raimundo Berenguer IV, as the legitimate king of Aragon, handed the castles of Monzon, Belchite, Barbara and Remolins over to the second master of the Temple. He added a tenth of the total rent paid on his lands and a fifth of all the territories that were recovered from the Moors in the future.

We can see that the prior decision to refuse the generous inheritance offered was a wise one, which ended in great gain for the Order of the Temple, a reward which nobody disputed and all believed to be fair compensation for the service carried out by the Templars. For despite demonstrating great efficiency in battle they also lost many men to the fight.

In the following years, the Templars fought in the battles of Tortosa, Lerida, in the siege of Miravet and in all the battles wagered for the recovery of the last remaining territories on either bank of the Ebro, from Mequinenza to Benifallet.

The desire of so many Spanish and Portuguese monarchs to create a military order similar to that of the Templars is easily understood. In 1158, Alfonso II founded the order of Calatrava, but the order of Montjoy had suffered so many failures that it ended up asking to be incorporated into the Templars. Once it had been accepted, the order handed over several valuable properties in the South of Aragon.

"...they may be few, but they have the value of many..."

With the passing of time the Templars in Spain became national, as happened with the master Gomez Ramirez, who was to die in the famous battle of *Navas of Tolosa*.

According to the account of Jaime I the Conqueror, we can calculate the approximate number of Templars that took part in the conquest of the island of Majorca. As soon as the conquest was completed, the lands and riches were divided among the victorious troops. The Order of the Temple received a twentieth of the booty, as well as a castle located close to the city wall of Palma. As the total of soldiers numbered around thirty thousand, we know that the Templars must have been about five hundred.

Jaime I respected their "excellent military organisation, the speed of their movement and the ease with which they were able to prevent any attack, as though they could read the enemy in the air or smell him, when he was yet invisible to the rest of the troops. They may be few, but they have the value of many."

The monarchs of Portugal were of the same opinion, and were very generous in their gratitude to the soldiers. They gave them the castle of Soure and the forest of Cera, and gave their permission for the founding of the cities of Ega, Radin and Coimbra, and the fortress of Tomar, raised on one of the most splendid areas on the banks of the Tajo. The fortress was begun in 1160, when Gualdin Pais was the fourth master of the Temple of Portugal, and was later converted into the Portuguese seat of the Templars. The building bore very characteristic features, as the monk-knights were also skilled in architecture, sculpture and other arts, and filled Spain and Portugal with many monuments of a particular symbolism, like a leaving card. Many of the monuments make references to superstition, to the Hebrews or the Muslims, while holding secret messages which continue to be studied today.

Just as in Spain, none of the property or land ceded to the Templars was given as a gift or as donations made to a religious order in devotion or faith. The gifts were always lands that had been recovered from the Moors or in payment for the defence of conquered possessions, when the enemy intended to recover the property with vicious attacks or by siege.

On the study of the Order of the Temple's actions in Spain and Portugal, historians have included a third condition to those of monk and knight: that of administrator. In the knowledge that land tends to generate more expense than profit, the Templars built mills, installed livestock, and cultivated the land, in addition to wine cellars, storage, smithies, dry goods stores and other sources of production being set up. The lands were rented out to labourers and farmers, to ensure an annual income.

They also imposed taxes, during times of poverty, on all the families who lived under the protection of their castles and fortresses. But they were never lenient with those who refused to pay, except in very extreme cases, as they had dictated laws that allowed the annulment of rent contracts in cases when the Order considered the delay in payment unjustified. This manner of administration that may seem cruel in modern times was quite normal in the Middle Ages, in a time when many other even harsher feudal rights were law, such as the armed retinue.

Of course the Templars were not free from taxes themselves on the properties they obtained, as can be seen in the kingdom of Aragon, where they were obliged to hand over a fifth of total profit. This led, at times, to large debts, though these were always paid off, often after winning a battle or receiving assistance from the brothers in other kingdoms around Spain and Portugal.

The Order of the Temple intended to support itself on the income, and be able to send large amounts to the Holy Land, which was indeed the principal motive for their existence.

San Juan of Mascoras

King Fernando of Leon took his troops, including a large number of Templars, to the heights of his land, from where they could observe the entire area. From there he initiated his attack on San Juan of Mascoras, in whose land many bandits and Saracens had sought refuge and were terrorising the inhabitants of Extremadura and part of Portugal.

The area was strongly defended and the enemy was knowledgeable in the art of war. But the army of Fernando doubled the enemy in number, were better armed and included soldiers such as the Knights of the Temple, who knew the strategy of siege, and in less than two days they successfully invaded the fortress. Once inside there was no hesitation in wiping out the few remaining survivors.

This conquest was the first of many, and Fernando II took total control of the entire Transierra region. In the following months he widened his conquests throughout Extremadura and along the banks of the Guadiana. The participation of the Templars was significant, and in gratitude he gave them the properties of San Juan of Mascos, Trebajo, Santa Maria of los Sequeros, Peñas Rubias, Torremilanera, Portezuelo, Alconetar, Esparragal and Coria. In almost all of these places the memory of the monk-knights has remained, mostly in the form of ruins, legends and documents that have become integrated into popular culture.

A merciful legend

Juan García Atienza, in his book *The Secret Purpose of the Templars*, says the following:

"With the castle of Ponferrada still in construction, the legend of mercy arose that sanctified the castle and gave it its divine air. It is told that woodcutters who were gathering wood for the beams of the Temple castle found an image of the Virgin Mary in the hollow of a tree. The image was believed to have been brought from Jerusalem many years before by Saint Toribio of Astorga, and there were even those who swore that the image had been sculpted by Saint Lucas himself. When the Muslims invaded, the image was hidden to safeguard it from the Moors, and all trace of it was lost until the woodcutters found it. With this story the image automatically became a religious relic, and in time the patron of all the Bercian territory that the Templars dominated, whose order had also been created in Jerusalem where the legend placed the origins of the image.

In a few years the soldier-monks controlled a territory that reached almost to Maragateria, El Bierzo and the mountains of Leon. Their farms, castles and lands given as payment extended from Balboa in the West to Rabanal del Camino, and in the East to Cerezal, bordering with lands of the Order of Santiago. Templar castles were erected in Cornatel, Bembibre, Balboa, and Antares, among many other places.

This story serves as testimony to the immense extension of land and property the Order of the Temple obtained in Spain, in gratitude for the efficiency demonstrated by them in the continuous battles of the Reconquest.

CHAPTER IV

THE FIRST BATTLES
IN PALESTINE

The Second Crusade begins

On 1st December, 1145, Pope Eugenio II proclaimed bulls of a new crusade. With respect to the errors made in the past, the leadership was entrusted to the King of France, Louis VII, who had made the offer of marching with a significant army to the Holy Land. One hundred and thirty Templars also joined the forces, under Everardo des Barres, the master of France and the future third general head of the Order.

The most passionate defender of the Second Crusade was Saint Bernard, whose words were so charged with motivation as to convince Germanic emperor Conrad III. He declared himself ready to ride at the head of a strong army to Jerusalem, which was not in the Pope's plans, as it was well known that the German emperor refused to take orders from the Frenchman.

The Germans decided to march by a different route from that taken by the Franks. They were the first to leave on the route that would take them across Hungary to the Byzantine Empire. Interestingly, the army commanded by Louis VII later followed exactly the same route, perhaps because they realised it would be easier to travel. However, near to Andrinopolis they were attacked by the Cumae and Pechenego people, whose wages were paid by Byzantium. Given that the enemy was in the Holy Land and not in their current location, the French king negotiated with the representatives of Constantinople, and was forced to pay a kind of toll. Once paid, his army crossed the Bosporus. His army had already lost a number of men, due to desertion and sicknesses, a common situation given the length and difficulty of the marches.

The proclamation of a great tragedy

When the French reached Nicea, they were greeted by a disappointing situation: the Germanic army had just been annihilated in Dorilea by the Turks, in exactly the same place where, fifty years earlier, the First Crusade succeeded in opening the way through to the Holy Land. Louis VII tried to maintain his troops' spirit, but the religious leaders met with more success with their preaching, as did the captains and their promises of doubling the wages of those who continued on the march.

From that point on it is worth taking a closer look at the great tragedy that followed directly from the first announcement of problems.

The French troops soon found themselves suffering from shortages of supplies. They had spent Christmas fighting, and in early January 1148 their route led them through a dangerous gorge. Then Godfrey of Rancon ordered his men to climb the most perilous face of the mountain. With this command he stopped obeying the orders of his king, Louis VII, who was delayed at the back of the troops and who had ordered that he wait.

The climb was arduous, and the army lost many soldiers and pack animals loaded with weapons and provisions. Hours later the army was able to set up camp behind some rocks, but the Christian contingent was on the edge of a deep ravine and the clouds were almost on them from above.

32

Suddenly Turkish troops appeared on nearby peaks, well-protected behind a natural wall of rocks. Godfrey gave the order to the archers to fire their arrows on the enemy, but the distance was too great and not one arrow reached its target.

It was growing dark, as shadow sunk upon them, the cold became their most dangerous adversary, and the hundreds of French troops found themselves at the mercy of the Muslim arrows and cutlasses. All were killed by the merciless soldiers or fell into the abyss in an attempt to escape or pushed by enemy hands. The screams of death, multiplied by the echo of the mountains, resembled a raging storm that left Louis VII and his surviving men deaf at the bottom of the ravine. The Christians were almost paralysed by terror, and might have perished there, had it not been for the rapid action of the Templar master Everardo des Barres, who maintained an order amongst his men while he consulted with the king:

"Your Majesty, we must await the morning," advised the shrewd warrior monk, "before the dawn I will find a path that will keep us at a safe distance from enemy arrows and falling rocks."

"I trust you, monsignor master," replied the monarch, his face creased in worry, "I know you fought in the Pyrenees against the Arabs and that you know the art of warfare in the mountains."

"You are right. Trust us, for as well as the lives of your army, your own and ours are also at risk."

Before the first rays of dawn lit the sky, the Templars had found the path to salvation. But not one of them left the ravine, bound by the oath not to desert and to obey the orders of their commanders, even though they may appear perilous.

The guide was a Templar soldier called Gilberto, who was given fifty horses to lead the way. It was soon clear that the route was completely free of enemy soldiers, though dangerous with rocky ground and narrow passages through which the horses and mules were scarcely able to pass.

The trek through the mountains took three days, and claimed the lives of tens of man and fifty animals. But finally they arrived at the port of Satalia, where the remaining men found salvation. Once they had eaten, drank and rested they received further bad news, which after such terrible events was almost easier to bear: they were not enough ships to carry them all.

Do not pay the enemy you leave behind

Louis VII negotiated with the Byzantine governor to grant an escort to Syria for the Christian soldiers that remained in his land. He paid a large sum of money and several chests of jewels in return for the favour, and later the troops that were lucky enough to be leaving bid farewell to those who stayed behind.

But as soon as the ships' sails had sunk out of view over the horizon all the Christians were taken prisoners. They were taken completely by surprise, having believed that they had been assured protection, and were not even able to draw their swords in defence. The younger soldiers were sold as slaves, and the older, sick or wounded men were forced out of the city and left to die of hunger and thirst. Unfortunately, none of the Christian leaders had known heeded this Muslim saying: "Never pay the enemy you leave behind."

The invaluable help of the Templars

It took three weeks for the king of France and his army to reach Antioquia, as they were delayed by storms. As soon as they disembarked they found that they had insufficient funds to buy provisions, and once again Everardo des Barres, the master of the French Order of the Temple, stepped in. He rode as fast as he could, without sparing his horses, to San Juan of Acre, and returned with money to purchase what they needed.

Louis VII would never forget the invaluable assistance provided by the Templars. His gratitude can be witnessed in the letter he wrote to his main treasurer:

"I have no idea how we would have been able to survive even another hour in this infernal country, had it not been for the help and advice of the Templars. Their master was always at my side, from the time when we set out from our beloved

34

land to the moment at which I am writing this letter. I therefore beg of you to redouble your sympathy toward this Order, so they may know that we have acted on this respect. Moreover, I advise you that the Templars have loaned us a considerable sum of money, which should be returned to them immediately, so that their house may be respected as a protector of the throne. We must not falter in fulfilling this promise, as such action would dishonour us all. I thus beg you to return to them with no further delay the sum of two thousand gold pieces."

The great failure of the Second Crusade

The Second Crusade only succeeded in prolonging the agony of financial assistance. The German emperor Conrad II, who had saved himself from the annihilation of his troops, arrived in San Juan of Acre with a new army. In the city he met with the barons of the Holy Land, including the notable master of the Temple Roberto of Craon.

However, the decision was made to postpone discussions until the arrival of Louis VII of France. Once he was present and the meetings were announced, it was discovered that the members were unable to reach an agreement on the first objective to be obtained, as they all had contrasting interests in the matter. Politics, in this case and in many to follow, was to be one of the most difficult obstacles.

After many weeks of discussion, the city of Damascus was chosen, and in July, 1148, the troops set out. On arriving, the army set up the siege of the city, choosing fields abounding with vegetation and fresh water, which was of great advantage to their side. However, though the reasons are unknown, the two monarchs decided to change the position of their troops to a desert-like location. It is possible that a group of inexperienced scouts advised that the city could be better held to siege from there, as the city walls were less fortified.

Time was to show the error of the decision, for all the attacks made on the city were held off easily by the Muslims, with substantial losses to the attackers. And to worsen the situation, word arrived that Muslim armies, with three times the number of soldiers than the Christians, were only two days away. And thus came about the great failure of the Second Crusade.

On abandoning Damascus, Conrad II set sail for Europe, followed shortly after by Louis VII. At that time the rumour of the downfall of the Templars was born. Some chroniclers of the time wrote of the betrayal of the Hospitallers and the Templars, sold to the Turks for three casks of gold coins. But as in so many stories of betrayal, built on fantasy and half-truths that result in tragedy or comedy, the rumours told that the traitors were conned, for when they opened the casks they found not gold but copper.

CHAPTER V

THE DESERTION OF
THE MASTER OF THE TEMPLARS

In the spring of 1149, Roberto of Craon, the second master of the Templars, died. His chosen substitute was Everardo des Barres, who was unfortunately at sea at the time and had to be elected in his absence.

Everardo marched alongside his king, Louis VII. Several weeks later, as soon as he arrived in Paris, he held a meeting of the Templars of the area, perhaps with the intention of bidding them farewell. However, before the meeting he received news of the death of one of his closest friends in battle, and it was the last straw in his desperation. He never returned to the Holy Land, and deserted the Order of the Temple to become a monk in an Order that renounced violence. He received many petitions to rejoin the Templars, but heeded none of them. He died in 1174.

Errors and bloodbaths

One of the first armed exercises of the Templars in Palestine was triggered when the Turks conquered the city of Tecoa in 1130. At that time Hugo of Payns was no longer and Roberto of Craon was the master of the Order. When news of the tragedy had reached him, from the few that had managed to escape the slaughter, he rode to the scene.

When he arrived, he found himself faced with a Dantesque battleground. The streets and buildings were strewn with corpses, smoke still rose from the blackened ruins of houses, the water in the wells was contaminated, and a putrid smell of death hung over everything. But instead of pursuing the Turks, in an attempt to prevent them reforming ranks, he decided to remain in the town. It was known that the invaders had left loaded with their booty, which would force them to travel at a slower pace, and also that they were likely to be drunk or exhausted.

The Order of the Temple was materially obliged to destroy the Turks, as they constituted one of the greatest threats to the routes of pilgrimage to the Holy Land. However, Roberto of Craon did not follow this obligation, and instead made the unusual decision to stay in the city. Owing to this decision, the confrontations with Turkish bandits became more frequent on the pilgrimages. Though the Templars were usually the victors in these confrontations, and only a few lives were lost.

Eleven years later, with Bernardo of Tremelay at the head of the Order, it was necessary to defend the fortress of Gaza, which was the last Christian battalion on the route to Egypt. The defence was accomplished with great efficiency, in the same way as the protection of the dangerous routes of the pilgrimages. The victory represented heraldry, which even the enemy recognised, though the Turks continued to be the principal threat.

In 1153, King Balduino III requested that the Templars besiege the city of Ascalon, as he was convinced that its conquest would result in the continuous attacks carried out by the Turks and other Arab nations ceasing. Bernardo of Tremelay had heard that in Ascalon a great treasure was guarded, and perhaps this was what drove him to execute an isolated attack with twenty of his best soldiers. The attack was suicide. The soldiers managed to breach the defence and enter the city walls. But when they were close

to where they believed the treasure to be, they were surrounded by a huge mass of enemy soldiers. They all died in
the fight, and their heads were raised on spikes and displayed around the city walls as macabre trophies, a tactic
used since the beginning of war to intimidate the enemy.

The legends are forged by extensive rumours

In 1154, the rumour spread through Palestine that the
Templars had betrayed an Egyptian prince in exchange for
60,000 gold pieces, even though he had been about to convert to Christianity. He was very soon assassinated by his
enemies.

Several years later, a dozen knights of the Order of the
Temple were hanged, found guilty of having given up a
fortress located on the other side of the Jordan to an Emir of
Nuredin without attempting to defend it. Almarico I himself, the new monarch of Jerusalem, dictated the punishment.

In those times Egypt was a constant battlefield, in which
the Templars suffered some of their worst losses: six hundred horsemen and more than twelve thousand foot soldiers. This encouraged them to consider signing a peace
treaty, taking advantage of the fact that two of the most
important Arab tribes, the Selyudides and the Fatimistas
were fighting at the time. The treaty was accomplished in
most precarious circumstances.

Soon the English Templars, Robert Mansel and Gilbert
of Lacy at the head of a reduced army, launched a surprise
attack on the troops of Nuredin. The victory was so overwhelming that the enemy ended up having to flee barefoot
without their horses.

Motivated by the triumph, Almarico III wanted to continue with an attack on the Sultan of Cairo, in breach of the
peace treaty. But he was only accompanied by the Order of
the Hospitallers (an Order similar to that of the Templars,
but who occupied themselves with matters of sanitation).
The new master of the Temple, Odon of Saint Amand,
refused to take part in the military expedition, as he considered it was doomed to failure.

Indeed, this is exactly what occurred, because the first defeats resulted in the signing of further peace treaties that allowed for Saladino's rise to power. He soon had all the enemy forces of the Latin Kingdom in the Holy Land under his control. The dozens of Sultans and hundreds of emirs must have seen a great quality in him to submit so much power, and they were not mistaken.

Was hashish introduced in the culture of the Templars?

Odon of Saint Amand, the eighth master of the Order of the Temple, was a very careful man who never made a step without being assured of beneficial results. Moreover, he gave his role as commander of a group of soldier-monks little importance, especially from a religious point of view. For this reason it is written that he even made pacts with the devil. Guillerme of Tiro wrote the following account:

"During Odon of Saint Amand's time as master, the chief of the Haxixin Sect, called Sinan 'the Old Lord of the Mountain', began to execute military action in the Arab lands. It was said that he ruled over more than 60,000 Ismaili villages, including the most feared warriors of the Islamic world. They had earned their fame by virtue of their great skill, an overpowering strength and a cunningness born from the desert fox. It was said that they achieved these qualities through the consumption of hashish, which also gave them the ability to take on the appearance of serfs or lords, as they wished, and to speak all the tongues of the area. Such prodigious advantages allowed them to enter the very home of their enemy and annihilated them cruelly. The Arab term *haxaxin*, from which we get 'hashish' is very similar to the modern word 'assassin'."

One day, Sinan sent his ambassadors to King Almarico I, with the promise to convert to Christianity in return for the liberation from the heavy charges that the sect had been paying as a tribute to the Templars since 1149. The monarch of Jerusalem accepted the deal, but when the ambassadors returned to the lands, laden with gifts, they were taken unawares by several Templar horsemen, who immediately killed them. This act was a great error. King Almarico was so furious that he demanded immediate compensation. He wanted the guilty men to be brought before him, but Odon of Saint Amand refused to comply, even when threatened with the abolition of the Order, and the situation ended in the siege of the Temple headquarters in Sidon. However, the king of Jerusalem died on one of the first nights of the siege, and the threat was removed. The Templars returned to their previous activities.

Legend tells that the Temple knights, who maintained their original western or Latin culture, started to consume hashish through their constant dealings with the sect of the Assassins. It is true that the fights between them were ceaseless, and also that on occasions, the study of a strong and respected enemy can result in assimilation of their tactics to defeat them.

The prohibited custom of consuming hashish, as well as that of dealing with Sinan and the other enemies that surrounded the Order, added to the Templars 'unmonk-like' behaviour, who only complied with their religious duties out of obligation or habit.

An exceptional leader

Saladino rose to power by assassinating a vizier and overthrowing the Caliph of Cairo, who was the last descendant of the Fatima dynasty. He was also careful to remove the fifteen year-old son of Nuredin, by seizing the cities of Damascus and Aleppo from him and forcing him to abdicate.

Almarico I's throne was succeeded by the fourteen year-old Balduino IV. The most surprising fact about this boy is that he was a leper. It is unknown how he became infected with the disease, but when he was crowned he was suffering from the initial stages, which meant that he was in his second or third year of the ten years of life that remained to him. Balduino was an exceptional strategist, and his armies faced those of Saladino on many occasions. He always counted on support from the Templars and the Hospitallers, and his most resounding victory is told by Alejandro Vignate in his book *The Enigma of the Templars:*

"Saladino lead his strong army close to Jerusalem, while Balduino IV was in further South in Ascalon, far from the main forces of his kingdom. As soon as he heard of the great risk to the Holy Land, he set off to face the Muslims with only five hundred soldiers, including eighty Templars brought from Gaza by forced march.

"He was prepared to wage war in the battle that the Christians called Montgisar and the Muslims Ramla. The Muslim historian Abulfaraje attributed the Christian victory to 'a sudden appearance of a miraculous wind, which blinded the soldiers of Saladino.' Certainly, the tale gave rise to a legend that survived many years in the land.

"The Christian version was quite different. Balduino managed to gather two thousand men, which he situated on the beach, hidden behind the dunes. When the Muslim army appeared, laden with booty having pillaged several nearby villages, and with no intentions of further combat, he gave the order to attack. The Christian horsemen rode like an unstoppable tirade. The Arab bugles sounded the call to battle in vain, for the Arabs were already fleeing. More than thirty thousand Arab soldiers were defeated that day, including the famed soldiers *Mamelucos*, who always dressed in saffron coloured silks that stood out amongst the other fighters on the battlefield.

"Those who managed to escape did so by crawling through the discarded helmets, weapons and shields that had been thrown to the ground."

The echoes of the battle spread throughout the world, with repercussions lasting many years. Saladino learned to think twice before attacking Christian possessions, and was forced to sign a peace treaty.

Balduino took part in the famous battle weak from his illness, and had to be tied to his saddle. But he fought bravely, and later went on to fight and triumph in many others, on occasions borne on a litter, until eventually he had to face the impossible battle against death, devoured by leprosy.

He died in 1185, only twenty-four years old. A few months previously he had authorised the construction of the Templar fortress Castle Vado, near Panias on the route to Tiberiades. On his death Rimundo III, the Count of Tripoli, was named Regent, as the legal successor to the throne was still a child, son of Balduino's half-sister Sibila.

What kind of bravery can be attributed to the Templars?

We have given enough examples to be able to answer this question, but despite this, historians are not in agreement. One group believe them to have been too proud, as though made of a special substance, and from a military point of view, this led them to behave recklessly. Of a contrary opinion are those who believe the soldier-monks of the Temple gained their cunning from so many years on the battlefield against the most skilful, wily and astute enemies in the world, and for this reason they were modest, brave and smart.

What historians do agree on is the Templars being unholy in their decision to follow King Almarico I of Jerusalem when he broke the treaty signed with the Egyptians. This action gave Saladino, the most feared enemy of Christianity, the opportunity to gather the most important Muslim forces under his control.

The controversy comes from the analysis of Guillerme of Sonnac's behaviour, as he was unable to stop the crazed Robert of Artois, the brother of Louis IX of France, who marched with only a small group of men to conquer Mansura. The Templars rode at his side, in the understanding that they were unable to desert him despite knowing they were riding to their deaths.

The Christians met with little resistance and managed to enter the fortress. But they had walked straight into a trap like mice to cheese. The entire Latin contingent was slaughtered, and as was the custom when an army respected the cruelty of its opponent, the heads of the leaders were displayed on spikes as trophies.

It is logical to argue that Guillerme of Sonnac should have refused to follow the lead of a madman, as another

Temple master had done years before, but we are faced with the sentiment of loyalty to the king of France, even if that involved following his brother to suicide.

It is interesting to view the other side of the numerous battlefronts that were waged in the Holy Land, particularly those against Muslim troops. All the events' chroniclers, without exception, sang the praises of the Templars' form of combat, who were considered the most disciplined, brave and prudent soldiers to have walked the earth; they started by acting like the fox, and became the desert lion, who attacks secure in the knowledge that victory awaits.

It is easy to feel drawn toward the Muslim chronicler, if we bear in mind that the Templars were always those who closed the retreat or formed the scout sweeps and the front line in combat. Thanks to them safe paths remained open on the pilgrimages for almost two centuries, for those who walked the way on foot, the caravans of provisions that supported the fortresses, and the gateway for the reinforcements that arrived in the Holy Land.

However, when we consider the level of friendship – a strange mixture of love and hate – that existed between the Arabs and the Templars, we are necessarily inclined toward the Christian chronicler, who described them as fearful soldiers.

A gift for the cruel Saladino

It was very hot in the city of Jerusalem, so much so that not even the Arab friends of the Christians nor their servants dared to go out in the sun. Only those who were forced by thirst to refill their jars at the city's wells were seen in the streets, and the city appeared to be sleeping, though who could possibly sleep with the vulture of war swooping over their heads?

Meanwhile, in one of the shady Temples of Solomon, around a table served with mint tea, dates and French wine, were King Raimundo IV of Jerusalem and Gerard of Ridefort, the tenth master of the Templars:

"I have considered it well, my lord," said the monarch in a hushed voice, not looking his interlocutor in the eyes, "we should allow Saladino to succeed in his siege of Tiberiades, and take the city."

These words brought the Templar to his feet, his face reddened, staring at the monarch and clenching his fists in desperation. "But... have you gone... mad?"

"No. Please, calm down, monsignor." But Raimundo IV's voice was weak and his pronunciation betrayed a certain insecurity. "I have had time to consider my decision these last days, since I heard about what is happening in Tiberiades."

"But do you realise what that would mean?" shouted Gerard of Ridefort, "Your wife and children are in the city! If we do not march there with the majority of our troops they will surely die!"

"I know, I know. Why do you reproach me so, my friend?" Tears were forming in the eyes of the indecisive monarch. "We are in the hottest time of year, the land we would have to cross is almost bare of wells, and it would be impossible to carry all that we need for the men and animals. We must wait for Saladino to come to Jerusalem, and walk into the trap we will set him.

"No no, your Majesty! Can you be so blind as to not see that such conduct would be taken as a demonstration of cowardice? Any father and husband would run to save his family, though there is only one chance in a thousand!"

Raimundo IV gave in to the pressures of the Temple master, little realising that he was facing one of his worst enemies, nor the intense hate that the Templar harboured for the weak but sensible king of Jerusalem.

The Christian troops set out in march under the burning sun. Their only hope was to reach the lagoon of Tiberiades as rapidly as possible, where they would be able to find enough water to think victory was possible.

When Saladino heard of his enemy's actions he could scarcely believe it. One of his spies, who must have witnessed the conversation between Raimundo and the Templar, arrived in all haste at the tent of his mater. A good horse, knowledge of the best shortcuts, and dressed in robes that had permitted his passing through a tight network of guards, he arrived with the most incredulous news. He was rewarded with a bag of gold pieces.

Can this be called a battle?

What followed has gone down in history as the battle of Hattin Hill, but in actual fact it was not much of a battle, unless that is the definition of thousands of men being marched to an inescapable end. They were forced to walk across a barren desert under the blazing sun, thirsty and barely able to see through the sweat that dripped into their eyes. They continued hour after hour, advancing painfully slowly and expecting the fall of enemy arrows at any moment. Unable to remove their heavy armour, the cavalry and the infantry had to set up camp right in the middle of their path. The lagoon at Tiberiades was still too far a distance away to think about.

There was a change of direction on two occasions, in the hope of finding wells with fresh water that tempted like a hallucination. When night fell, it was sufficiently cool to raise the spirits of the men a little.

The march was restarted an hour before sunrise, when suddenly Muslim archers appeared on horseback. The Templars set off in pursuit, but they were forced to draw back after a little way in case they were being led into a trap. They had just reached their men again when they saw the flames and columns of smoke. The Arabs had set fire to the dry scrub, and a smell breeze drew the flames toward the Christians. Panic set in among the foot soldiers, and they ran off in all directions, many of them attacking the horsemen that tried to retain them.

Then Saladino gave the order to attack. The cavalry were without the protection of their archers, and they were forced to use their shields. But their horses made easy targets, and finding themselves horseless, thirsty, hot and tired, the men ran for protection to the hill of Kafr Hattin, where they found the king of Jerusalem and an enormous cross. They were unable to defend it.

It is calculated that some fifteen thousand Christians

found themselves at the mercy of Saladino, whether put to death or sold into slavery. Almost two hundred and fifty Templars and Hospitallers fell foul of the executioner's axe.

However, the capricious Muslim chief left the king of Jerusalem alive, as well as some of the barons of the Holy Land and Gerard of Ridefort, the master of the Order of the Temple. This was perhaps as a reward for handing him the entire Christian army, and as a consequence, the city of Jerusalem.

CHAPTER VI

THE FALL OF JERUSALEM

The plotting of the master of the Temple

If we go back in history to before the famous meeting between Raimundo IV and Gerard of Ridefort that led to the massacre of Hattin Hill, let us take up the latter's story.

Gerard was the authentic medieval adventurer, forged in palace intrigue, a man of a thousand faces and a surprising ability to fool those around him. As soon as he arrived in the Holy Land he made his services available to Count Raimundo of Tripoli, who had not yet been named Regent of Jerusalem. From this position, Gerard fixed his sights on Lucia, the heir to the castle of Botron and the favourite niece of his lord.

Raimundo of Tripoli gave him the support he needed to ensure their wedding, but at the last moment a shortage of money forced him to change his mind and marry Lucia to a rich man from Pisa who promised a large sum of money in return.

Faced with this abrupt change of plan, Gerard had no choice but to grit his teeth and bear it, despite the fact that the marriage would have gained him entry into the nobility of the Holy Land. This is the root of the hatred that the master of the Temple would be dominated by in the future, something which nobody could have foreseen. At about that time he left Jerusalem.

For a long time nothing was known about his movements, until he appeared in the Holy Land with the position of the king's Major General. The schemes he must have carried out to achieve such a high position are unknown.

But we do have evidence that he became ill and requested that the Templars care for him. The Order had a private hospital and succeeded in curing him, and as he showed great religious dedication during his time there, never missing a single service, and even praying from his bed when he was too weak to be moved, he was allowed to make the three vows of admission. It could have been that he was feigning the illness in order to obtain a high military and religious position. In 1184, he was named seneschal of the Order of the Temple, and a year later, on Arnaldo of Torroja's death, he was elected master, the highest position.

Arnaldo of Torroja was born in Spain, where he was the son of nobles, and died in Verona at the end of 1184, while in the process of conducting a mission as ambassador of the Order in the European courts. His work as head of the Templars was considered moderate, if not sufficiently ambitious for the demands of his most important collaborators. It is possible that the choice of Gerard of Ridefort, for the vote was in secret, was due to his sharply contrasting character: the Templars wanted an ambitious, restless leader who would be able to adapt to the tumultuous life in the Holy Land.

Gerard's election took place when Balduino IV was about to die from leprosy, and Raimundo of Tripoli, the sworn enemy of the tenth master of the Temple, was regent of the kingdom of Jerusalem.

Gerard of Ridefort was busy plotting for more than forty months. He made no direct accusations, but he allowed his advice to be heard and laying evidence of the weaknesses of Raimundo IV, in order to build a support of important allies.

The crown will not go to my enemy

Gerard was at the bedside of the young king when he finally died. He immediately took charge of all the necessary rites, and the embalming and dressing of the corpse. Once all the rituals had been meticulously adhered to, he ordered that the body be placed in the coffin.

Lastly, in the company of ten of his most loyal Templars, he organised the moving of the coffin from San Juan of Acre to Jerusalem. When the procession arrived there, his allies were waiting for him, along with the princess Sibila, who was to be crowned, in a ceremony involving several important people including the patriarch of the Holy Land.

Raimundo IV, the sworn enemy, was in Naplusia, and when he heard of proceedings he sent a messenger to impede the coronation. Another obstacle in the master of the Temple's path was that the crown of Jerusalem was kept in the Holy Sepulchre, which needed three keys to open the great door.

Gerard of Ridefort had one, the patriarch of Jerusalem another, and the third was kept by Robert of Moulins, the master of the Order of the Hospitallers. At first Robert of Moulins refused to hand over his key. He even fled from Gerard in order to make it clear that he would not comply. Though his character must have been weak, as when he realised that the master and other noble men were in his pursuit, he threw the key to the floor in a rage and shouted:

"You cannot force me to be present at a coronation ceremony that is against the wishes of the deceased Raimundo IV!"

But Gerard of Ridefort had got what he was after, and on 20th July, he watched from a privileged position the entire ceremony that converted his favourite, Sibila, into the queen of Jerusalem. "The crown will not go to my enemy," he was heard to whisper, "This has compensated for my failed matrimony with the heir of the castle of Botron."

However, things had not gone entirely as he had planned, as the most important noblemen in the Holy Land continued to consider Raimundo IV as the only legitimate king of Jerusalem.

On the brink of the great massacre of Hattin

Gerard of Ridefort was unable to follow up his plans, as Saladino had once again entered into action and in the Holy Land the only thoughts were war or peace. This was the preoccupation of Raimundo IV, when he succeeded in putting a stop to the hopes of conquest of the cruel Muslim leader by signing a treaty. This gesture in truth was no more than that, but at least it enabled the people to live some months of calm.

Meanwhile, the master of the Temple had obtained a great ally in the form of Guido of Lusiñan, queen's husband. The two were on the brink of sending their armies against the castle of Tiberiades, where Raimundo IV was to be found, but the threat of Saladino prevented their actions.

At the beginning of 1187, the Christians broke the treaty when they took control of an Arab caravan. Saladino was enraged and demanded immediate compensation: the handing over of the guilty parties and the return of all the booty. When the Christians refused, he soon organised one of the strongest armies to be seen in the history of the Holy Land.

The huge Muslim army was an obvious threat to the Christians, to the point where Guido of Lusiñan and Raimundo IV put their rivalry over the crown aside to talk. Guido sent a delegation, headed by the masters of the Temple and of the Hospitallers, who had now forgotten the confrontation concerning the third key to the Holy Sepulchre.

While negotiations were being held, Raimundo IV was informed that an Arab detachment was preparing to cross the territories of the Tiberiades. As there had so far been no action of war, apart from the attack on the caravan, he ordered that they pass freely.

Gerard of Ridefort then made a traitorous decision. But instead of going directly to his enemy, he opted to go straight into action. He and eighty Templars armed themselves with the best weaponry, took the best horses from the stables, and he convinced some ten Hospitallers and forty knights to join them. Before this small army left the fortress, Roger of Moulins, the master of the Hospitallers, tried to detain them:

"You are going to face forces that are ten times superior to your size. I beg you to stop this madness immediately!"

"The master is right, monsignor," interrupted Jacquelin of Mailly, one of the valiant Templars, "I think it is worth reconsidering your orders."

"I will not, cowards!" shouted Gerard, enraged, "And if you, my companion of the Order, do not agree, you may dismount and give your weapons to your foot soldier, for I have no need of you!"

"I will go with you, my lord monsignor, for my sense of duty obliges me. I limit myself only to expressing my opinion."

This must be considered an anecdote, if we compare it with the battle that was waged in a place called Fuente del Berro where the Christians suffered a bloody defeat, despite all of them giving up their lives in a great show of bravery. What is notable is that Gerard of Ridefort escaped alive. Perhaps because the Arabs pardoned his life in the hope that he would concede them similar favours in the future.

This event appeared not to awaken Christian suspicion, as the crafty master remained in his position after recounting the occurrences of Fuente del Berro. However, he had been unable to prevent the reconciliation between Raimundo IV and Guido of Lusiñan.

Moreover, as proof that he was prepared to fight Saladino, he offered to hand over the 'treasure of the king of England' in order to be able to recruit a powerful army.

The so-called treasure of England was a large quantity of money and jewels that Henry II had given to the Templars and the Hospitallers, in a ploy to achieve the Church's pardon for the assassination of Cardinal Thomas Becket. However, he was specific in his request that the treasure should not be touched until his arrival in the Holy Land. The master of the Temple did not respect the king's conditions, perhaps suspecting that the king of England would never reclaim it.

Gerard was able to recruit a significant number of men, though fewer than he had hoped due to the refusal of the master of the Hospitallers to open the chests of the treasure from England that his order guarded.

At this point, it would be a good idea to take another look at the events of the last chapter and the massacre of Hattin Hill. It seems a relatively obvious conclusion of the events of the bloodbaths of both Hattin Hill and Fuente del Berro, to see that Gerard of Ridefort handed the lives of thousands of Christians over to the cruelty of Saladino.

Jerusalem surrenders

The massacre of Hattin left Jerusalem undefended, which meant that the religious patriarch of the city had to organise his frightened neighbours, who were in dire need of guidance in their desolation. Not a single family had escaped the loss of one or more of their own in the recent battles, but the need to protect the young and the old made them react to the crisis.

Days later, the knight Balian of Ibelin, one of the few whom Saladino had allowed to live, arrived at the walls of Jerusalem. He had been wounded, but he had recovered well, and was mounted on a horse saddled in the Arab style. Everybody understood that he had been sent by Saladino as a negotiator, something that sparked a glimmer of hope.

Indeed, the Muslim leader had let him live in order to render him this service. The soldier was the bearer of safe conduct, with which he assured that the lives of his wife and children would be saved in exchange for obtaining the immediate surrender of Jerusalem.

Balian was determined to carry out his mission, but the people started to beg him to help them defend the city, as he was the only one with any military knowledge. He was forced to accept, and later, when he saw the scarce defences available, he spoke with the patriarch and the ancient nobility about organising the surrender of the city, if only to save Jerusalem the agony of a siege.

Saladino had calculated everything down to the last detail: ten gold pieces for each man, five for each woman, and one for each child. The payment was given a period of forty days, under the threat that anybody with no money would be sold as a slave. For the poor people, a sum of thirty thousand coins was established in exchange for the lives of seven thousand of them.

54

At this point Roger of Moulins did open the chests of the treasure of England, to cover the sum demanded for the poor. But there were far more than had been calculated, and so there was not enough money for everybody.

On this occasion Saladino kept his word, perhaps because the money he did receive satisfied his greed. In actual fact, he allowed all the inhabitants of Jerusalem to leave, and made a second surprising concession: he did not punish the traitor Balian of Ibelin, who was made military chief of the holy city for the few remaining days, when it was understood that he had been forced to comply for the sake of his wife and children, whom he loved more than his own life.

This is one of the contradictions of such bloodthirsty people, who are also capable of being generous and kind. As far as the poor of Jerusalem are concerned, it is estimated that about ten thousand of them were saved, but many more were left, and their fate is unknown.

The flight of the refugees was organised into three groups, commanded by the Templars, the Hospitallers and Balian of Ibelin. They were protected by about one hundred and fifty Muslim horsemen, well selected by Saladino to avoid any possible conflict with Arab people they may meet on their way.

When the refugees arrived in Tripoli they assured that the surrender of Jerusalem had been executed peacefully. The fate of the Holy Land was to take a new turn from that moment.

Saladino in Jerusalem

In October, 1187, Saladino arrived in Jerusalem with his entire entourage. Straight away he gave orders for the most important buildings to be cleaned with rose water. He personally organised the removal of the golden cross that crowned the cupola, and wielded the first axe blow to destroy the altar inside. Later, he ordered that the Temple of Solomon be converted into the mosque *al-Aqsa*, and he knocked down the wall that blocked the view of the *mirhab*, which was a sign to show the direction of Mecca.

A *minbar* was constructed, which resembles a Christian pulpit, to serve as a reference for prayers. The mountains and lands that surrounded the city were also purified with rose water. However, all that remained was respected, for Jerusalem was, according to the writings of the Koran, one of the most beloved places of all faithful Muslims.

CHAPTER VII

IT ALL COMES TUMBLING DOWN

The end of Gerard of Ridefort

There remained nothing more of the kingdom of Jerusalem than a reduced coastal border and a few castles and fortresses. The Christians concentrated on defending the Tiro peninsula, as most of their fortifications were almost totally impregnable. It was there that Conrad of Monserrat landed at the head of a small fleet.

Little is known about this man. He took over the control of operations straight away, with so much enthusiasm that he refused to receive Guido of Lusiñan, who had been released by Saladino on the condition that he never again raised his sword against the Muslims. He was forced to ride with it tied to his saddle for all to see.

Gerard of Ridefort was given similar orders, though he did not respect the imposed conditions. He went to the strongly guarded fortress of Tortosa, where he saved the lives of his men when all appeared lost. They resisted in the face of certain defeat, and managed to hold off the enemy.

However, the master of the Temple received no support.

He was considered a traitor, and it is likely that they were waiting for calmer times to remove him from his position at the head of the Order. But before that could happen, the traitor was killed in San Juan of Acre in a heroic fight, as though he were trying to purge himself of his guilty conscience.

The fight that took place succeeded in motivating the Templars and the other knights to do the impossible and resist the attacks of Saladino's forces. The Muslims suffered such great losses that they were ordered to retreat and abandon the battle. But by then Gerard of Ridefort was already dead. It is believed that he died on 4th October, 1189.

The eleventh master of the Temple

The Templars went almost two years with no master, perhaps due to the fact that they had to face the problems of day to day survival against the permanent combat with the armies of Saladino. The election was finally held during the planning of the Third Crusade, and this may have been the reason behind naming Robert of Sable, who was a friend of Richard the Lionheart, the king of England.

Robert of Sable had been a gentleman, married twice with three children. But he gave up all family rights when he entered the Order, first as a guardian and then as a brother, where he gained the respect and admiration required to obtain the highest position.

The decision was also influenced by the fact that the new master of the Temple had reached the post of admiral in the English navy, and had served as an intermediary for several princesses of his country in matters of heritage. All these responsibilities he abandoned on entering the Order and converting himself in soldier-monk. Years later, when the Knights of the Temple met to hold their secret election, there is no doubt that Sable's previous activities held him in good stead as an able negotiator and to prove his honesty. The complete opposite could be said of Gerard of Ridefort.

The Templars' powers of recovery

Despite the huge expenses that the recruitment of the armies had entailed, the Templars' safes were still full of money. The treasure of England had never been reclaimed, as Richard the Lionheart had forgotten it when he arrived in the Holy Land. He very possibly had no knowledge of it at all.

Strangely, the English king chose to conquer Cyprus before taking part in the Third Crusade, and then sold it to the Templars for a vast sum of money. The negotiations were concluded very fast, which gives the impression that the Templars did indeed possess a surprising ability of recovery, above all where their finances were concerned.

It should be pointed out that the Templars now had immense riches at their disposal in the main cities of Europe, for they had become the bankers of many royals and nobles, and large sums constantly arrived in the Holy Land. They also possessed significant donations from monarchs and nobility, such as the treasure of England, which were paid in compensation for serious political or military errors, or any other conflict involving the Church.

The start of the Third Crusade

Again there were two kings in charge of the Crusade. However, this time they were the king of France, Philippe August, and Richard the Lionheart of England. As was becoming tradition, before embarking on an immediate recuperation of lost territories, they found themselves submerged in the conflicts that followed the death of Queen Sibila in 1190.

Months of negotiation were spent choosing between Guido of Lusiñan, the widower, and Conrad of Monserrat, who had just married Isabelle, the younger sister of the queen. In the end, Conrad of Monserrat was elected, which so annoyed the Templars that they broke the agreement for the sale of Cyprus. Richard the Lionheart used the situation to make a present of the island to the loser, for his

59

favourite candidate had won, due to the influence that he had exerted on the circumstances. He was a great politician as well as an able war strategist.

Finally the Christian forces were able to devote themselves to the duties in the Holy Land – recovering the lost territories. Despite the matters of the palace, they had maintained a series of skirmishes and small conflicts, in response to the attacks that they suffered continually at the hands of the armies of Saladino.

They took almost two years to conquer the city of San Juan of Acre, which finally surrendered in 1191. The talks, and the later signing of the papers that closed the battle operation, were held in the tent of the maser of the Order. Months later, the king of France returned to his country, leaving the French troops under the command of the Duke of Borgogna.

The night that Richard the Lionheart roared in rage

Saladino's emissaries arrived unexpectedly at San Juan of Acre, bearing a document that requested negotiations. Nobody had forgotten the massacres of four years earlier, still remembered in many masses. Another surprise was that the Christians worst enemy in the Holy Land asked for the Templars to intervene to act in releasing the three thousand Muslims who had been taken prisoner in the recently conquered city.

Again confusion and doubt reigned. Those who did not deal with the Templars on a daily basis viewed the love-hate relationship between the Christians and Muslims as suspicious. Robert of Sable possibly refused the request on the advice of Richard the Lionheart, and the release of the Arabs was never executed.

However, there was a further, more severe obstacle to the negotiations: a sudden burst of anger from the king of England, who ordered that all the Muslim prisoners be sentenced to death. There were actually two thousand and seven hundred of them, and not one was left alive, in an act of revenge that little reflected Christian ideology, but which gave the crusaders enough courage to set the wheels in motion for their vengeance on Saladino for each of the defeats suffered at his hands.

Another massacre like Hattin?

The march was begun on 23rd August, 1191, with a bigger and more determined army than any seen before in the Holy Land. The Templars marched at the front of the troops, as they knew the terrain well from their many years defending it, and the Hospitallers brought up the rear. It was said that scrub grew so tall that it reached the foot soldiers' beards.

They soon met with Muslim horsemen, whose arrows had always been infallible. But this time they found the enemy prepared, and were forced to retreat or face high losses. The Christians lost the greatest number of men in the river of crocodiles, when some men could no longer face the merciless heat of the sun and the exhaustion of the march.

Once across this river, the attacks of the Turks became more frequent. For three days the Christians were subjected to a terrible assault, already suffering from the burning sun and intense hunger. It was told that they were even forced to eat the injured horses. And all feared a repetition of the massacre of Hattin.

On 7th September the open battle began, though historians are not clear on who first gave the order to attack. It could have been a minor command, looking for a more noble death than that of waiting for the enemy arrows to strike.

On this occasion victory favoured the crusaders, who then continued their advance toward Jaffa. It took them three weeks to cover a distance of some sixty miles, for they had to care for the wounded and bury those killed in the battle. Moreover, the land was rugged and threatened ambush, and many times the troops had to wait while scouts assessed the land.

Saladino leaves the terrain free

When the army reached Jaffa they found it in ruins, and they had to set up camp in the streets. Fortunately the fruit trees had not been destroyed, and the men were able to feed themselves on figs, grapes, almonds and pomegranates, and they also found livestock that had escaped from the city and nearby villages, which gave them an abundant supply of meat.

They soon heard that Saladino was in Jerusalem, and with no obvious signs of planning any counter attack. Richard the Lionheart, the Templars and the Hospitallers were not reassured, however, as they knew the swiftness with which their enemy could change its mind. They continued their advance, passing many of their old fortresses, castles and other fortifications, all destroyed.

Several of these places were cleaned and the troops attempted to rebuild some sort of defence from the ruins. However, the work did not raise the king of England's morale, and he expressed his grief at his failure to gain the Duke of Borgongna's confidence, he himself still in command of the French army. The army also faced constant attacks from Arab marksmen while they were forced to advance through the city's ruins, from which they had not a moment's rest.

Such low state of morale may well have been behind the decision to advance to the city of Jerusalem, the recuperation of which had become the symbol of the trophy of the Third Crusade. They needed to triumph in this conquest to satisfy the other monarchs of Europe and the Pope himself.

Even the weather was against them

The first three days of January were chosen for the initiation of the advance to Jerusalem. They all knew that the twenty miles between them and the city would be laden with traps amongst the rocks and gorges, perfect ambush terrain. Again the Templars took charge of the scouting missions, to ensure the safe passage of the rest of the troops.

But on the afternoon of the first day the sky joined forces with the enemy. Black clouds darkened the air, and a storm of rain and hailstones destroyed the tents where the king and the knights were sheltering, ruining the provisions, drowning many horses and mules, and rusting much of the weaponry and armour.

The weather so threatened the Christians that Richard the Lionheart had to call off the advance. The recuperation after the storms would take many weeks, and as he no longer had such a large army he decided to postpone the attack on Jerusalem, where Saladino awaited them with well fed and prepared troops, that tripled his own in number.

Desertion and political games

The king of England mistrusted everybody, and thus had not wanted to take the masters of the Temple and the Hospitallers' advice when they tried to convince him that advance toward Jerusalem was pointless. In fact, he always bore in mind that he could well be betrayed by either one of these religious orders, though this thought must have been erased from his mind some months later when he had to abandon the Holy Land, as we will see further on.

Richard reached Escalon with his army. The Muslims had also left this city in ruins. If this was a source of relief to the English king, it was soon countered by the news that most of the French troops were abandoning the crusade.

After so many months away from home, having seen a huge number of their colleagues die, and with the recent disaster of the storms, many of the soldiers had decided that God himself had abandoned them. Most of the deserters were moreover wounded or sick, had lost all their possessions, and were only left with the faint hope of finding the cure for their ailments far away from this unholy place, if they could manage to reach their homes alive.

But then a political change seized the Christians' attention from their aims of advancing over the Holy Land: one of the 'Old man of the mountain's' Muslim assassins had killed Conrad of Monserrat, the king of Jerusalem, which meant that a successor must be appointed immediately.

As was the custom in the western courts, the plotting began as soon as it was realised that the two candidates had almost equal claims to the throne. Richard the Lionheart backed Count Henri of Champagne, who was to be the triumphant party, and who was forced to marry Conrad's widow Elizabeth to reinforce his position.

The escape of Richard the Lionheart

The dice were thrown, despite the fortress of Darum having being triumphantly besieged and conquered. Richard the Lionheart only nourished the sensation of loss, which was being strongly criticised in the European courts. He acted with great diplomacy, having resisted Saladino's attacks in Jaffa, in signing a three-year peace treaty. This allowed the Arabs to recover Escalon and Darum, while they swore to give free pass to all the pilgrims who came to the Holy Land.

One day Richard received a letter that filled him with dread: his brother assumed the king to be dead, and had taken the throne of England. He had to leave Palestine as soon as possible, but feared that he would be murdered on the way. His only hope was to request the assistance of the master of the Temple, whom he did not trust:

"I beg you to forget past conflict between us," pleaded the king to Robert of Sable, "for I need your immediate help. Ask your knights and sergeants to escort me under cover to my country, where I will present myself disguised a member of the Temple."

The king was asking for an almost shameful escape, not appropriate of a monarch called Lionheart for his courage. The master of the Temple gave his approval, and planned the voyage with the highest secrecy, which allowed him to consider the departure of such an important person.

Richard left in a galley belonging to the Temple, for the fleet that they had in the Mediterranean.

What was impossible to avoid was that the ship was forced to pass close to Venice, driven by a storm. There, Richard changed from his disguise as a Templar to a merchant's garb, bid farewell to his companions and set off for Vienna. Weeks later he was taken prisoner by King Leopold of Austria, who held him captive for several years in the hope of claiming a ransom. What happened afterwards is part of the legend told of Sir Walter Scott.

What remained of the Third Crusade

The Third Crusade was a total failure, although it did give the Christians an area of safety along the coast, from Antioquia to Jaffa. The European monarchs and the Pope must have been satisfied with that, for they took almost one hundred years to organise the Fourth Crusade.

In 1193, Robert of Sable died. It can be said that he always acted with great prudence and diplomacy, as was expected of him. To these virtues can be added his qualities as a treasurer, for he duplicated the money of the Order in both Europe and the Holy Land, and obtained hundreds of new properties.

With one of those coincidences that history occasionally throws up, that same year also saw the death of Saladino, the Sultan who had caused most damage to the Christians in the Holy Land. On his passing years of peace reigned, as the Arab courts were occupied with the rights to succession. Many tribes had sworn allegiance to the powerful leader, but when he died they attempted to ensure leadership for their own chiefs. Long disputes, including several assassinations, gave the Christians time to occupy themselves with maters aside from the military.

As for Gibert Erail, it is known that he carried out the management of the Temple in Provence and Spain with great ability. In Spain he earned particular prestige when he demonstrated that the bad news that had reached them from the Holy Land would have no effect on the battles waged there against the Arab occupation, in battles in Valencia, Zamora and Portugal. Proof of the respect that he gained in the country is seen in the gift of a new castle made to him and the Temple by the king of Aragon.

To the Templars the start of the Third Crusade signified further wealth, more property and almost total independence. They were not even obliged to inform the king of Jerusalem of their activities, nor did they have to dedicate homage, mass or oaths to him.

The new master of the Temple had to face the tough Castilian nobility, and was convinced that the higher grade of independence he could achieve the easier it would be for him to act. He went to the new Pope, Innocence III, who granted him his collaboration, to the point at which he converted Gibert of Erail and his successors in a type of absolute monarchs: they had the power to do with the donations received, benefits obtained, and all the property as they wished, be it for religious or social use. They would never again have to defend their accounts to the Pope.

A year later, a bull announced that a bishop had no right to excommunicate a member of the Temple. The bishop of Tiberiades wanted to excommunicate the entire order, when he was refused access to a large quantity of money that his predecessor had deposited with them. The Pope intervened, and named two ambassadors, the bishops of Sidon and of bibles, to resolve the conflict.

After many weeks of talks, neither of the parties was able to reach a compromise, until one Sunday the bishop of Sidon was so disgusted by proceedings that he completely excommunicated all the Orders of the Temple at the mass held in the church of the Holy Cross of Tiro, including all the Templars on both sides of the Mediterranean. The parishioners were left speechless at the bishop's outburst.

The Templars went to the Pope, who decided in their favour, and accused the bishop of Sidon of showing signs of an unmeasured pride and wickedness inappropriate in a representative of the Church. The punishment for having dared to stand against the Temple was completed by the removal of the bishop from his position.

So the results of the Third Crusade were not so bad for the Templars, as they came out of it stronger than ever, and they certainly made the most of their reinforced position in the time between the third and the Fourth Crusade.

Chapter VIII

THE GREAT POWER OF THE TEMPLARS

The master of the Temple never forgets

In 1191, King Leon of Armenia took the castle of Gastein, which had been taken from the Templars in battle four ears earlier. The appropriation was considered the booty of battle, though he had found the place undefended. But due to conflict between dynasties, the events went almost unnoticed.

But eight years later, when Leon of Armenia requested the Templars' help in his struggle against Count Bohemundo of Tripoli, the first thing that Gilbert Erail did was show him a bull signed by Pope Innocence III stating the right of the Templars to reclaim the castle of Gastein.

The ambitious monarch of Armenia who had just converted himself and his people to Christianity, not only promised to return both the castle of Gastein and a second in Darsebac, but also offered his nephew Rupin as a pupil to the order.

The master did not reply until he had heard all the conditions of the offer. As soon as he realised that the monarch wanted him to intervene in conflict against another people of the area who had also converted to Christianity, he rejected the military agreement and prudently retired from the negotiations. Hours later, before dawn, he took all his cavalry and foot soldiers from the city.

Time always favours the strongest

Leon of Armenia requested the help of the Pope to force the Templars to assist him. On receiving the answer in the negative he ended up forming an agreement with the Hospitallers, who offered their collaboration in exchange for several important fortresses and castles, not including Gastein.

Gilbert Erail died in 1201, leaving the memory of a man whose work demonstrated his diplomatic and persuasive qualities, and his good relations with the European monarchs and the Pope. The matter of Leon of Armenia was considered a failure too small to blot his otherwise highly prestigious record with the Templars.

His successor was Philippe of Plaissiez. We know little about the twelfth master of the Temple, apart from his inadequate management throughout the eight years he occupied the position. He managed to provoke a significant number of knights of the Temple broke their allegiance to the order to enlist in that of Cister.

This was one of the worst periods for the Templars, if we ignore its ending. As the underlying problem with Leon of Armenia was still latent, the Pope sent two cardinals to act as judges on the matter.

While the judges were on their way, Leon's army attacked Antioquia, where a group of Templars was residing. None doubted a moment in standing against the attack, employing battle towers, the fiercest catapults, and both infantry and cavalry. In the face of the size of the attacking forces, the Templars again demonstrated their abilities as fearsome soldiers.

The defeat resulted in Leon seizing all the properties that the Templars had in his land, though he failed with the castles of Roca Guillaume and Roca Roussole, as they were so well defended that his troops were unable even to reach the walls.

The arrival of the two cardinal-judges was a relative triumph for the Templars, as they excommunicated Leon of Armenia for refusing to return the properties, and for his unjust conflict with the count Bohemio of Tripoli.

However, the monarch refused to accept the decision and once again went to the Pope with new pleas of help. Meanwhile, Philippe of Plaissiez died in 1209. Few mourned his death, and his successor was immediately named as Guillerme of Chartres, who had been in the order for sixteen years and had donated a large amount of land before taking his vows.

The thirteenth master soon showed his qualities as a diplomat, and was able to calm the anger of the high people of the Holy Land. They were all demanding action against the count Bohemio of Tripoli due to him contracting the assassination of the patriarch of Antioquia the year before. The crime should have earned him excommunication.

Fortunately the Templars had not assisted the count in recent times, though they had in the past, and faced no accusations of anathema.

In 1211, the Order of the Temple went to war against Leon of Armenia, in response to his continued attack on the castles of Roca Guillaume and Roca Roussole. They were helped by a small force lent to them by the king of Jerusalem, all experts in open warfare. They were confidant in facing the enemy and well equipped.

However, they were ambushed while crossing a seemingly peaceful gorge. The scouts had declared the way safe, and the ambush left many Christians wounded, including Guillerme of Chartres and several Temple knights. One knight died in the place without being given his rites of death.

Many small battles followed, which were brought to an end when Leon of Armenia surrendered in 1213. As proof of his defeat, he returned all the properties that he had seized from the Templars and begged the Pope himself to absolve him from his multiple sins. But he was unsuccessful in his pleas, and moreover was obliged to give up his throne to his nephew Rupin. In spite of his efforts to make up for his sins he was left desolate.

The Order of the Temple obtained more than their property in Armenia and several chests of gold pieces, as the region became once again the most powerful and influential Christian stronghold in the Holy Land. They continued to obtain further riches and property in the area, for the strongest always wins in the end, provided he does not rest on his laurels.

The great pilgrim castle

It could be said that half the world lived in or around a castle, which had even taken over from the great monasteries and abbeys. But their maintenance required large expense, and for this reason those of the Holy Land had been kept by donations, which had failed to materialise in more than forty years. What is more, the castles had been shown to be vulnerable in the face of attack.

As the Turks were constructing a great fortress on Mount Tabor, which would dominate some of the principal pilgrimage routes of the Christians, Guillerme of Chartres made the most important decision of his reign: to build a castle that would have the best defences, possess all the means of auto sufficiency, and also include the most splendid religious, military and social facilities.

The first to suggest the castle was the king of Jerusalem, after having tried unsuccessfully on various occasions to conquer the Turkish fortress on Mount Tabor. The master of the Temple chose the place on the summit of Athilt, which would allow for the control of all the routes of passage to Haifa. The Templars had already erected a tower in the area, which they called the house of the straight. It was situated on the edge of a natural inlet, which permitted the arrival of important shipments of supplies.

The best reference to the work is found in the writings of Oliver the Scholastic, from which here we can see the most descriptive pages:

"High over the sea a headland leans, quite wide, which provides natural defences on three of the four cardinal points. There is an old tower constructed by the Templars... The building work had no more than started when a hidden treasure was found, which when opened contained ancient large golden coins, which the generosity of Jesus Christ must have buried there to assist in the huge expense.

"In excavating a second wall, the labourers hit a source of fresh and abundant water, in the form of an underground stream.

"The towers constructed stretched a hundred feet into the sky, and measured sixty-four thick. A space was left for a double wall.

"The whole building now encloses a chapel in the interior of a palace, next to which a large number of domestic constructions have been built. This meant that the convent of the Temple could leave the dirty and sinful city of San Juan of Acre and take up residence in the new castle to await the reparation of the walls of Jerusalem.

"The whole area includes fisheries, salt mines, a small wood, a meadow, cultivated fields and sufficient pasture to feed hundreds of cattle and horses. The orchards and fruit trees will also provide a harvest for those who wish to eat their produce.

"The new castle has been the cause of alarm in the Muslim villages, which are now almost deserted. As the castle is also located only a few miles from mount tabor, the Muslims have been forced to abandon the fortress that they had erected on its peaks."

The magnificent construction was called the Pilgrim Castle, as it was at the side of one of the main pilgrimage routes. It was built on a headland of nine hundred and eighteen feet by eight hundred and fifty three feet, and was a majestic architectural work, a completely self-sufficient city, well protected, which suffered its first attack in 1220, when work was still to be finished. It bore the attack with almost no damage, and was never to be conquered by the Muslims, until it was abandoned when considered no longer useful, and left to the elements and time.

The huge wealth of the Templars

The Order of the Temple built many other castles, such as the fortress at Safed, thanks to the generosity of donations. It was usually the work of bishops and Popes, though, who pressured monarchs, nobility and the rich bourgeoisie into complying with their obligations. Not only did they stop making payments to the collection, but they also forgot the interest on the loans made by the Church. But in the end everybody paid their debts, in fear of being excommunicated.

Another source of income came from the continuous pilgrimages, some of which used the ports built by the Temple in Marseille and other Mediterranean cities, as well as the ships and wagons provided by them.

In order to gain some idea of the Templars' great expenses in the Holy Land, it is suffice to say that within the fortress of Safed alone nearly two thousand people ate every day in times of peace, as well as eighty Temple knights, fifty horsemen and their mounts, three hundred artillery men, almost nine hundred pages and sergeants and some fifty slaves.

The Templars possessed some fifteen similar townships in Galilee, Lebanon, Syria and Armenia, as well as supporting the convents of Tripoli and Antioquia, the caravans, and around five hundred Temple knights with their entourage. They must have had something that resembled a multinational industry to be able to cover the costs of it all. And that goes without mentioning the thousands of properties in Europe, the banks and the hundreds of Temple knights and innumerable individuals who collaborated in one way or another.

We cannot forget another important source of income that the order had assured: the constant pilgrimages to Acre and Tortosa, the two cities that had replaced Jerusalem. The first of which had a port, a palace and a church, which provided enormous benefits. However, more than eighty per cent of this wealth came from the second, the beautiful Tortosa of the Holy Land, which belonged almost in its entirety to the Templars. These sharp businessmen had converted each alley, building, church and square into a religious relic, similar to the principal tourist areas of the Mediterranean today.

On certain occasions it was also possible to take pilgrims to the city of Jerusalem, when peace reigned and with the authorisation of the Muslim people, who continued to be a source of worry. The Templars made money from these activities, though they had to share the profits with the Arab nation.

Preparation for the Fourth Crusade

The Fourth Crusade was the work of the Popes Innocence III and Honorio II, who managed to secure twenty per cent of the Church's total income for the task. To administrate such a significant fund, brother Aymard, the head treasurer of the Temple of Paris, was selected.

In November, 1217, the king of Hungary, the duke of Austria and a large number of important knights arrived in the Holy Land. They all brought strong armies, which however did not prove very efficient in the first battles.

The majority of them gathered at Castle Pilgrim, from where the first attacks were organised. Oliver the Scholastic also arrived, and wrote some interesting chronicles and accounts of the events of the Fourth Crusade. Through his writings we have been able to discover what took place in Egypt, on the banks of the Nile and outside Damieta. The Arabs had pulled a giant chain across the river, in order to impede the passing of the galleys and other important ships:

"The Templars chose a sailing ship for the expedition, in which travelled forty brothers and other people, and a total of three hundred men. They waited a few moments until a strong breeze arose, then they rowed against the current. Their intention was to crash into the chain and break it, but at the moment of impact the Arabs of the city and the tower started to fire arrows and other weapons upon them.

The attack was so strong that the helmsman lost control, and the ship was driven toward the city. When the Christians realised what was happening, they lowered the sail and threw out the anchor, which left them stranded in the centre of the river. They were soon boarded by the enemy, who numbered over a thousand. The Templars who had retreated under cover saw the impossibility of winning against so many, and prepared to give their lives in the service of Our Lord. Thus they broke the bottom of the ship, so that it sank, taking with it more than a hundred and forty Christians and approximately one thousand five hundred enemy soldiers."

The task of crossing the Nile turned out to be such a problem that the crusaders took over ten months to achieve it. When the Christians besieged Damieta it was discovered that the Arabs possessed catapults and other battle machines that were capable of launching stones, heavy blocks of metal, bales of burning straw and other weapons from a great distance. This tactic destroyed a large number of assault towers, and those that remained whole could not be pushed up to the walls under the rain of arrows from the enemy archers.

As well as these fearsome weapons, we must add another, which had nothing to do with the Muslims but was produced by the terrain they inhabited. It was a strange disease similar to scurvy, which wiped out the Christian troops. The disease manifested itself in gangrene in the gums and in the bones in the arms and legs.

One of the many affected by this mysterious illness was Guillerme of Chartres, the master of the Temple, whose command over the troops had been excellent under all conditions. He was substituted by Pedro of Montaigu, who had been master of Spain and Provence, and came from a noble Valencian family.

The conquest of Damieta was not enough

The huge losses suffered by the Christians did not stop them holding the city to siege, and eventually the Arabs started to lack provisions, and the Sultan Malek al-Kamil offered conditions of peace: he would hand over the kingdom of Jerusalem, except Crac and Montreal, if Damieta were freed.

The crusaders held animated talks on the offer, for the European leaders were prepared to accept the deal, but the majority of those representing the troops who were familiar with the situation in the Holy Land did not agree. For them the conquest of Damieta would mean an almost complete cease in the Muslim attacks from Egypt.

Finally the decision to refuse the offer was made, and

some months later, Damieta surrendered. When the crusaders entered the city, they found the place in absolute desolation: the dead had managed to kill the living with the infection of the plague that they carried. In every square, house and mosque the corpses were piled up, but giving the impression that they formed part of a respected family or social group, for they were embracing or very close to one another, as though they had tried to protect the others in the last moments of their agony.

In those times the plague was combated with fire, and so all the bodies were dragged to the flames and their remains buried in deep graves. But this Dantesque scene was not the only thing found by the Christians: they also discovered an authentic treasure trove of gold, silver, ivory, jade, silks and other valuable items, all of which was shared out amongst the armies. Lastly, the mosque was turned into a church.

The conquest of Dametia allowed for the exploration of the Nile, without finding significant obstacles, as the people of its banks were too frightened. Even the military detachments proved to be afraid, for the castle of Tanis was discovered abandoned by the Turks.

But neither this news nor others of similar kinds succeeded in raising the morale of the Christian soldiers, for their chiefs could not reach an agreement on how to continue with the campaign. The wait stretched out, resulting in several months of idleness, which brought pillage, drunkenness, laziness and the demonstration of almost all the capital sins. The conquest of Damieta had not been sufficient for those who had gone to the Holy Land to fight for the recovery of the entire place.

The legate Pelagio, bishop of Albano

Pelagio was of Spanish origin, and he acted like an authentic leader, despite the fact that he had neither military nor financial experience. The worst of the situation was that he represented the Pope, which means that all the enormous amount of finances that arrived from Europe must have passed through his hands. Suffice to say that only in 1220 the treasurer of Paris, the Templar Aymard, sent more than fifty thousand marks to the Holy Land. This money was enough to maintain almost all of France, including the clergy and the army. Of course the brother was reprimanded by the Pope for his generosity, as on occasions he duplicated the sums that he had been ordered to send to the other side of the Mediterranean.

This huge sum of money enabled the crusaders to improve their standard of living, though there was still no fighting. Meanwhile, news arrived of the continuous Arab invasions of various fortresses, which resisted attacks due to provisions still getting through.

Gradually, the Christian leaders started to abandon Damieta, as they were not in agreement with the behaviour of the legate Pelagio. Juan of Brienne, the king of Jerusalem, was the first to go, and he was followed by several important nobles, and finally the master of the Temple himself, who justified his decision to leave in a letter:

"A certain pontifical legate comes to preach in the churches, with the full support of the clergy, that an open war should be organised, because he believes that with a few simple charges our problems will be resolved. But the army chiefs, both those at sea and in the Holy Land, know that we do not have sufficient forces to abandon Damieta. The Sultan of Babylon has constructed bridges across the Nile, and fortresses along its banks, in which thousands of troops await us.

"The legate preaching has undermined the crusaders' confidence. As I can find no way of making him change his opinion, I am forced to leave the fortress. Our only hope lies with the arrival of the German emperor and other great knights, which will provide the reinforcements that we so need."

Chapter IX

A CHAIN OF FAILURES

The surrender of Damieta

The occupants of Damieta were disappointed to find that the arrival of German ships did not bring the emperor himself. Instead they brought the Duke of Bavaria, accompanied by other nobles from his country. As these reinforcements were not sufficient, the Templars, the Hospitallers and the other knights of the Holy Land agreed to accept the Sultan of Babylon's conditions. They surrendered Damieta in exchange for all Jerusalem except for the fortresses of Crac and Montreal.

But the papal legate and the duke of Bavaria, along with the king of Hungary and other important European leaders, wanted to resist. The reasoning can be summarised in these words:

"We have not come this far to remain sat on our laurels while such conditions are discussed that would offend the entire world."

In the end, the will of these so-called 'people of the high seas' won through, with the help of a constant stream of letters that arrived from the Pope and various kings, who complained about the lack of military action. The last word was had by the king of Jerusalem when he showed up with four galleys laden with knights and weapons.

The Christian army left Damieta by ship, to sail up the river Nile. On one of the branches of the river they found the first of the Sultan of Babylon's encampments. They moored up on the bank and started to set up camp. But the morale of the men was low, and ten thousand men deserted while the army was there.

The forces were therefore reduced by more than a third, and the chiefs could not depend on the rest of the remaining men to fight with the necessary discipline. Then the Arabs opened secret gates in the river, and the water level started to rise, and for some reason particularly the water around the bank where the Christian army was camped.

The men tried desperately to escape from the trap, but they lost all their provisions, the pack animals, and part of the weaponry. They were completely trapped, with no ships, provisions or weapons, and a huge lagoon between them and the enemy.

They had no choice but to accept the primitive conditions, which had they accepted before, could have saved thousands of lives and an incalculable sum of money, with all the equipment lost. However, the Sultan of Babylon also accepted the agreement, for he could have struck the definitive blow to the Christians of the Holy Land.

The Sultan did many other favours for the crusaders: he returned Christian prisoners being held in Egypt and other Muslim countries, and provided food and water to all those in Damieta for a period of fifteen days, after which time the Christians had to surrender the place that had cost them so many months of siege. The events were a total failure, which put an end to the Third Crusade. As usual, the majority of those responsible for the action tried to lay the blame on others. Pedro of Montaigu, the fourteenth master of the Temple, was one of the few that faced up to his responsibilities.

The sad arrival of the excommunicated emperor

In 1227, the Holy Land received the news that Friedrich II, the German emperor of Sicily, was about to arrive with more than forty thousand men. But in the end, the whimsical monarch changed his mind and returned to Brindisi. His doctors sent letters excusing his actions to the Pope, but they were not taken into account.

Gregorio IX had been waiting for such a long time for the emperor to join the crusade, that in the face of the most recent failure he made the decision to excommunicate him. This meant that the forty thousand German soldiers who had reached the Syrian coast had to turn around and leave again. Only eighty knights remained, under the command of the Duke of Limbourg, who were determined to enter into combat, despite the ten-year peace treaty that had been signed with the Sultan of Babylon, extending until 1230.

In order not to give courage to the Muslims, who had taken fright at the sight of so many armed Germans, it was decided to fill the time by reinforcing the walls of some of the castles, such as in Cesarea and Jaffa. This would also ensure that the troops did not remain inactive.

The dilemma of the Templars

The Templars found themselves up against a great dilemma: they knew that the emperor Friedrich had been excommunicated, but he had some right to the throne of Jerusalem due to the fact that he was the tutor of his son, Conrad. The master Pedro of Montaigu decided to remain slightly withdrawn and await developments of the situation.

But this was an impossible position to take against the actions of such a heartless man, who had dared to sign a peace treaty with the Sultan of San Juan of Acre. Despite showing everybody the papers, nobody believed him. However, they were forced to accept the facts when he rode to Jerusalem with a large entourage and a significant army.

Once in the holy city, he prepared the church of the

Holy Sepulchre for the event, and then he proclaimed himself king, in flagrant disrespect of his own son's rights. His swift actions left little opportunity for anybody to remind him that having been excommunicated the ceremony was completely invalid.

Just like a furtive thief, the emperor Friedrich left Jerusalem the following day, forgetting his promises to rebuild the city, eliminate all the changes installed by Saladino, and fully establish the presence of the Christians in the city.

The truth concerning the treaty was soon discovered. Jerusalem was obliged to be a city open to two religions, both Christian and Muslim, and the Temple of Solomon, of which the Christians dreamed, would continue to be a Temple to Mohammed. Still worse, the fortresses located around the holy city were to remain under the control of the Sultan of San Juan of Acre. To this the Templars were forced to react, and with their swords raised they challenged the king:

"Leave here, Sir, or you will end up in a dungeon for the rest of your life!"

The proud man returned to his ship, swearing vengeance under his breath. The Knights of the Temple must have understood that it was necessary to reinforce the defences of the holy city, and made use of donations they had received to begin fortifying several castles.

The emperor Friedrich was so angered by their actions that he demanded an immediate meeting outside the city of San Juan of Acre. There he greeted Pedro of Montaigu with some of the worst insults he had ever received.

"Sire, I do not believe that we are deserving, my holy Order and the humble servant who has the honour of directing it, of the insults you throw at us," replied the soldier-monk, in a calm voice, "I only say to you that we will not break any peace treaty, and our intentions are only to make certain repairs."

The emperor's answer was made by his actions, for he ordered his men, all German, to surround the gates to the city of San Juan of Acre and fire upon any Templar that dared to try and enter.

But the situation with Friedrich II was now untenable, for his last actions against the Order of the Temple made all his men deserving of excommunication. For this reason, on 1st May, they left their post, amongst the insults rained upon them by the people in the port, shouting:

"The Lord wishes you never to return, damned excommunicates!"

Friedrich was humiliated by this failure, and confronted with such he reacted by concentrating his anger in the form of hundreds of letters that he sent to all the chancelleries of Europe and to the seats of bishops, accusing the Templars of maintaining treaties of brotherhood with many of the Sultans, of attending ceremonies held in the mosques, of wearing the clothes of Muslims and smoking hashish, as well as claiming that the symbol of the cross had been exchanged for the half moon of Islam, amongst other wild allegations.

His accusations were not taken seriously, at that time. However, they were to be taken from the archives years later, when the Order of the Temple had to face the most merciless of tribunals.

Armando of Perigord, the fifteenth master

The master Pedro of Montaigu died in 1232, leaving a legacy of discipline, integrity and diplomacy. He was succeeded by Armando of Perigord, who had been master of the Temple in Sicily and in Calabria, where he was accustomed to following a policy of provisional action, under the ideology of 'act today, and tomorrow God will command'. The strongest advantage that he provided, if indeed it can be considered an advantage, was his friendship with Juan Ebelin, the aged leader of the Cyprians, who acted against the emperor Friedrich II, and who took the habit of the Order weeks before his death in 1236.

He was buried in San Juan of Acre, but he left an enormous unfilled space in Syria, where he had been the leader of the Christians. The position had to be filled, over the course of the following turbulent years, by the patriarch and the masters of the Temple and of the Hospitallers. However, the triple command ended up in the confrontation of the two most important military Orders.

Historians have recorded that the Hospitallers and the Templars fought hand to hand, set lethal traps in dark alleys for each other, and brawled constantly. All were motivated by the confrontation between their leaders. While the Temple wanted to sign an agreement with Damascus, the Hospitallers chose to sign with Egypt.

When the resulting war that had erupted in Cyprus came to an end, however, the situation was calmed, and the soldiers returned their swords to their sheaths and put their strength and thoughts to more practical use.

A heroic death

The Templars were once again in the middle of political change, having signed treaties with the Sultans of Damascus and Hons. This enabled them to recover the valued Temple of Solomon and carefully restore it, ignoring the threats of Friedrich II, their worst enemy of the time. They cared little that he threatened to confiscate Temple property in Germany and Sicily, for they were well guarded and protected.

Four years of prosperity followed, in which the soldier-monks reconstructed the city of Safed and other fortifications. They believed themselves to be the most powerful force in the Holy Land, for they were consulted by all sides on important decisions and all the while donations continued to arrive from all over Europe.

But suddenly, like the sharp pain of a heart attack, loomed the threat of the Mongol armies. They were already devastating the lands of Hungary, Prussia and Poland, and they had far superior weapons than the Christians. Moreover, the troops were used to riding great distances, and they possessed a new war strategy known as 'the pliers'.

The European kingdoms and the Pope were taken by surprise, for they had always believed that their only enemy was the countries of Islam. Remembering the scourge of Attila, and faced with the terror of their people, they found no way of reacting to the threat. It was told that the army had annihilated hundreds of thousands of people, and that they were advancing like flames through dry bush land. They were now located near to the coast of the Adriatic.

But then the threat disappeared, with the death of the Mongol leader in the Asian steppes. Endless masses were held in thanks, and the lips of thousands of Christians moved in grateful prayer. But the situation did not last long.

The threat arose of attack from the Carismenios, a Tartar tribe that had abandoned its land under the attack of the Mongols. They launched their first attack on Jerusalem, where the master of the Hospitallers was killed, as well as hundreds of knights and thousands of innocent people. They also desecrated the Holy Sepulchre.

The threat of these barbarians seemed directly aimed at the inhabitants of the Holy Land, and so the Christians and the Muslims joined forces against them. The battle began in October 1244.

The Carismenia and Mameluke forces had united under Beybers, who had risen from a Mongol slave to Visir. He was later to become the Sultan of Egypt.

The Holy Land had never faced such a situation, for Muslims were now fighting Muslims. Perhaps this was why the fighting was more vicious, and the soldiers only retreated to avoid a mortal blow or because they had lost their mount. Blood flowed over the ground, and the screams of agony were mixed with those of victory, in both Arabic and European.

When the Muslim troops allied with the Christians retreated, the Christians advanced, in keeping with the agreement made before the battle. It was soon clear who would celebrate the victory, for fresh Carismenia and Marmeluke soldiers sprang out continuously from behind the rocks, the hills and the thickets. But the soldiers fought bravely in the face of such strength.

Armando of Perigord perished on the battlefield, along with three hundred of his men, two hundred Hospitallers, and many other Christian soldiers. The new master of the Hospitallers was taken captive. Among the survivors were fifty-two members of the two military Orders.

CHAPTER X

THE SEVENTH CRUSADE

The purest king

In 1248, when King Louis IX of France left his country in a Genevan and Pisan fleet, he was accompanied by his wife, Queen Margaret and his brothers, Robert of Artois and Charles of Anjou, as well as many other family members. All set off desiring to take part in the new crusade, which would be the seventh. They took the island of Cyprus as their military base, some days' sail from Egypt.

The Emir Beybers had taken Damascus, Gaza and other important cities, and was showing himself to be the undisputed lord of the Holy Land. The Christians needed to recover Damieta and then march to Cairo, for there was no doubt that the conquest of Egypt would mean the end of all Muslim attacks on the Holy Land.

The Templars had been without a master for some time, for the death of Armando of Perigord had not been confirmed. His place was temporarily covered by Jean of Roquefort, who was soon officially replaced by Guillerme of Sonnac.

The seventeenth master maintained good relations with

the most important Sultans of the area. It was told that he was made welcome as a guest in the emirs' palaces for long periods, where he adopted their ways, to the point at which his lifestyle resembled that of an infidel. This formed part of the dark rumours that undermined the Temple's foundations, though it did not appear to affect its members to any great degree, as they unwittingly continued to nourish the danger that assaulted them at their roots.

Guillerme of Sonnac attempted to convince the king of France to make some type of contact with the Sultans of the area, particularly with those who had taken the side of emir Beybers. But he was met with the following reply:

"Never will we make deals with infidels! I hope you bear that in mind in the future, monsignor! And I will tell you something else – I do not want to find out that you have received any Turkish emissaries without my authorisation! You must always consult us, never forget that!"

It must be pointed out that King Louis was a most holy and saintly king, but a useless diplomat. In territories that had been at constant war for centuries, where on countless occasions political interests had been more important than religious matters, it was hardly advisable to reject any possible alliance, even with the devil himself.

But the king of France never accepted that theory, and refused to make an alliance with a strong Mongol leader who was prepared to fight at his side against the Muslims. He heard the Asian ambassadors, but only to make them the offer of conversion to Christianity. He refused to show any interest in sharing arms or fighting alongside the Muslims.

A victory deserving of the gift of Damieta

The departure of the ships to Egypt was delayed following a storm, after having had to overcome the disputes between Genevan and Pisan ship owners. In May, 1249, the Christian leaders met to finalise the plan of attack on the fortress of Damieta.

They reached their objective at the beginning of June, and found themselves greeted by more than ten thousand

Turks, on horseback and on foot, well-armed with cut-lasses, daggers and other hand weapons. The hordes launched themselves into the water with the intention of boarding the Christian ships. They seemed prepared to fight without any consideration of a treaty.

But they were held off by a superior force, which had the advantage of shields and protective armour. Some of the Christians were even able to descend on horseback, and the crossbows also went into action. The battle raged for over eight hours, until the Muslims were overcome from all sides and forced to retreat.

The Christian losses were few, while the Turks lost more than five hundred men and a large number of horses. The victory was well-deserving of a mass, which was held in an improvised church on the beach. Louis IX led the prayers of gratitude, in which the satisfaction with such a good start to the Seventh Crusade was attributed to the powers of God.

To top off the celebrated battle, the following morning they discovered that the city of Damieta had been abandoned. They immediately raised the standards of the holy king on the city towers, and the ships were used as bridges to allow hundreds of Christians to enter the fortress. All celebrated the victory, and took great pleasure in re-converting the mosque into a cathedral dedicated to the Virgin Mary, and named a city bishop. The sound of the chant of 'Te Deum' accompanied their labour.

The buildings of the fortress were shared out between the Templars and the Hospitallers, and the Pisans and the Genevans, and as they were the owners of the ships that had helped assure the conquest, they were allowed to build a market and several streets for their businesses. Indeed, they were a merchant people rather than sailors.

After some days, Queen Margaret arrived with Balduino II, the Emperor of Constantinople. During that summer Damieta became the capital of the high seas. But the inactivity began to demoralise the soldiers, and the people suffered from African diseases and food shortage.

There had not been room inside the fortress for part of the Christian forces, and they had to set up camp on the banks of the river. Provisions soon arrived, along with money to pay the wages owed to the soldiers. Thoughts were turned to sailing up the Nile, but they were in the flood season, when the fields of the delta were sunk and the current dragged many trees and obstacles that would impede the ships' progress.

The plans would have to wait until September, which meant that they missed a good chance of attack, for the Sultan of Cairo was failing. The Christians knew the news, and attributed the Muslims' inadequate reaction in the face of invasion to the fact that they had been missing one of their most important leaders. But they were unable to take advantage of the opportunity as a result of the impossibility to advance up the Nile. They were forced to wait, with the added problem of the troops' restlessness.

The advance into the unknown

On 28th November, the advance was launched. The majority of the troops marched along the bank, accompanied by the fleet of galleys. But progress was very slow, rowing against the strong current, and they only advanced one and a half miles a day. Meanwhile, the Turks observed from very close by.

The Templars brought up the rear, as usual, and were therefore responsible for holding off the first attacks. They took almost a month to reach the outskirts of Mansura, at the place where the Tanis flows into the Nile. A jetty was constructed to close the canal, but when they put it into the water it was carried away by the current. Worse still, the infantry who were trying to fix it to the banks were wiped out by the arrows of the Turks and the Marmelukes.

So the crusaders fell back on the tactic of wheeled assault towers, which were made of wood and quickly burned by the enemy's catapulted missiles. Louis IX's troops were frightened at these tactics, and the Templars, familiar with this type of warfare, had to try to reassure them.

The Christians were in fact facing two great strategists, Fakr al-Din and Beybers, who had already defeated the Christians in Gaza.

On about 8th February, the crusaders took a Bedouin to the tent of the king. He claimed to know a type of attack that would get them out of the trap in which they found themselves. The master of the Temple mistrusted the collaborator from the start, despite the considerable sum of money in question. But the other leaders of the crusade accepted his offer.

So the troops set out into unknown territory, as they discovered when they found that the passage was via a wide branch of the river, which nearly drowned more than a hundred soldiers on crossing. The water came up past their waists, and in places the current was so strong that it dragged away the weakest and made the laden horses impossible to manage.

Once on the other side, they counted over fifty men lost, as well as many provisions. On top of this, the Bedouin had escaped. The crusaders were so enraged that when they came across a group of Turks, the count of Artois gave the order to attack them. The master of the Temple Guillerme of Sonnac advised that they could walk into an ambush if they marched after the enemy in unknown terrain, but once again the other leaders waved his concerns aside, for the proud French monarch considered himself far superior to a Temple master, who was in fact his official military inferior.

The poignant letter of Louis IX

There is nobody better to recount the story than the words of Louis IX himself, in a poignant letter written to his court in France. Here we include the most important pages:

"On the following day we ordered out troops into battle and headed for the ford. We crossed the river in the face of great danger, for it was deeper and more difficult than we had suspected. Many knights had to swim across. Neither was it easy to climb out on the opposite bank, which was covered in mud. After overcoming these obstacles, we reached the place where the Saracens had prepared the machines across the path that we wanted to take. So our vanguard attacked the enemy, and many people were killed, regardless of sex or age. The Saracens lost a chief and several emirs.

"As we had dispersed, we were able to reach the village called Mansura, where we killed all the Saracens we came across. But they realised the imprudence of our soldiers, and regrouped their forces, took courage, and launched a counter attack that surrounded our soldiers and annihilated them. Many of our barons and soldiers were slain, both the religious Orders and others. We also lost our brother the Count of Artois, whom we shall remember eternally.

"The Saracens attacked us from all sides with a shower of arrows. We tried to resist their violent attack until nightfall, when our missiles ran out and we were left to their mercy. With many soldiers and horses wounded, we managed to maintain our position only with God's help. As soon as we were able to regroup, we tried to reach the place where the Saracens' machines were.

"We made a bridge of boats, so that those on the other side of the river could cross. We were able to destroy the terrible enemy machines, and the others were able to cross and join us. We were only few, but we were certain that we would be victorious in the end.

"On the following Friday, a huge number of the children of perdition attacked our lines. The clash was more terrible than anything seen before in these lands. With God's aid we held strong on all sides, and resisted the enemy, killing great numbers of them.

"Some days later the Sultan's son reached Mansura from the western provinces, and was received by the jubilant Egyptians. I believe his presence doubled the morale of his soldiers, for from then on everything took a turn for the worst in our camp.

"We were also victim of a contagious sickness, which killed off men and animals. But there were few of us to mourn the death of these lost companions. I must also add the problem of hunger to the tragedies that befell us, which was beginning to have the same affects as the sickness. The provisions had long ago stopped arriving from Damieta. We discovered later that two caravans were attacked, all the food stolen and the Christians murdered.

"Our total lack of supplies sowed desolation and terror in our army. We decided to retreat to Damieta, but as the paths of providence do not depend on man but on He who directs our steps and enforces His will, on 5th April we fell into enemy hands, with much Christian blood spilt in the fight. Most of those who were returning to the river were killed or taken prisoner. I must state that they all showed great courage. Nobody retreated and all fought until resistance was no longer possible. I believe I lost consciousness at some point."

Extra ransom money

What Louis IX told in his letter took place over a period of forty days. Along with the Count of Artois, Guillerme of Sonnac also perished, after losing his remaining eye (the first was lost in a previous battle). More than two hundred Templars, three hundred and fifty Hospitallers, almost five hundred Frenchmen and many others were also killed.

It was written that the fish in that part of the river turned carnivorous and devoured the remains of the corpses, for there were so many that they formed a bloody surface on the river where the current flowed more slowly.

The Sultan that so animated the Egyptians and the Marmelukes was Turunshah Ayub. He was a chief with so much experience in river warfare, that he gave the order to build dozens of lightweight boats, which were borne by camels to the banks of the Nile, where they intercepted the caravan of ships that carried provisions to the king of France and his thousands of men.

The surrender of the Christian troops on 5th April was not due to the decision of Louis IX, as he was gravely sick and unable to speak. What is told in the legend is that a French captain who had bribed a Marmeluke emir spread the rumour among the hundreds of survivors that the holy monarch had ordered a surrender. The identity of the traitor was never discovered, and it is possible that there were many who assisted in spreading the rumour, who wanted to escape the situation any way they could and were unaware that they were promoting a lie.

Another event that Louis IX failed to include in his account was the immense quantity of money that had to be paid for the rescue of the Christians. It took several days to weigh out the coins, jewels, precious stones and other valuable objects, and when finally counted, the caskets containing the ransom filled a large room.

As a closing line to the story, there is a small anecdote: the Saracen weapons included a type of incendiary bomb, which was catapulted and exploded into fire that was almost impossible to extinguish. Many Christians fell victim to this weapon, and it took several years to find the way of resisting the bombs.

Problems of conscience

Despite having paid the enemy more than three hundred thousand pounds, the sum of thirty thousand pounds was added, but the crusaders' safes were empty.

The Christians went to the Templars, as it was well known that they had large sums of money due to their role as bankers in the Holy Land. Esteban of Otricourt, the man in charge of the Temple funds, was summoned to the king's tent:

"I am sorry, your majesty," said the monk-knight, "I am obliged, due to a sacred oath, to defend these funds with my life. I may only hand them over to the hands that entrusted them to me. If you can convince these noblemen to authorise the employment of their funds, I will be freed from my responsibility."

Louis IX's counsellors examined the list of investors to see if the owners of the money were in Europe or in other places far away from the Holy Land.

"You are not freed from you oath", determined the holy king, who was still recovering from the illness and reclined

94

on a couch. Take the funds as a loan, which will be returned in as short a time as is possible, with the interest that you impose. You have the word of the king. Does that appear sufficient?"

"My lord of France, you may rest at ease," interrupted Rinaldo of Vichiers, the Major General of the Temple order, and the highest authority on the death of Guillerme of Sonnac. "You may have the money as soon as you wish, for we have overlooked that you have entrusted property in San Juan of Acre to us, as well as certain sums, which we can claim to cover the sum that we hand over to you now."

So the problem of the ransom was resolved. But the decision of Rinaldo of Vichiers was embarrassing for his future, as under no circumstances was it permitted to use clients' money without previously consulting the assembly of Temple knights in charge of the finances of the Holy Land. Moreover, the act of claiming the properties and money in San Juan of Acre turned out to be more difficult than first thought, due to complicated administrative procedures, having to find buyers, and seeking the approval of the Temple administrators of the city.

Finally the situation was resolved, due to the fact that the Major General of the Temple was supported by all his colleagues, and some months later was given the position of master of the Temple in a unanimous secret vote between the knights. He was also the godfather of Louis IX, as queen Margaret had given birth to him in Pilgrim Castle.

When the Temple was humiliated before the holy king

Louis IX was the highest authority of the Church while he was directing the Crusade, for he was the representative of the Pope. That meant that the Templars and the other Christian Orders and forces were under his command. Of course it was always possible to offer advice, though the king had the last word.

Despite the resounding defeat in Mansura, the king was received as a hero. He remained in Palestine for almost two years, during which time he had to resolve many complicated cases, including one that was related to the Templars and their custom of secret relations with the Sultans of the area. We can allow Jean of Joinville, the personal biographer of the king of France, tell the story:

"Brother Hugo of Jouy, who was then the Major General of the Temple, went to visit the Sultan of Damascus in the name of the master of the Order, with the intention of obtaining the sum corresponding to some land. Negotiations were carried out in this manner, imposing the condition that the king was in agreement. After a while, the brother returned accompanied by an Emir, the ambassador of the Sultan, bearing a document.

"The brother recounted the events to the king, who became very angry, and warned the Templar that he had been reckless in establishing relations with the Sultan without previously consulting him. The king finally agreed that the matter should be resolved, and so he raised three corners of his canopy, thus making the matter public knowledge. Many people arrived, including the master of the Temple and the entire convent, mostly barefoot.

"The king ordered that the master and the ambassador of the Sultan be seated before him, and demanded of the master in a loud voice, 'Monsignor, I want you to tell the ambassador that you are ashamed of having opened relations with the Sultan without having previously consulted with me! And as you have never uttered a word of this to us, I free you from all responsibility assumed, and I return the signed documents to you.'

"The master took the documents and gave them to the emir, saying: 'I am returning these to you because I have acted wickedly, for which I repent.' Then the king asked the master to stand up, and to give the order for all the brothers to do the same. As they did so, he declared the following: 'Kneel before me to repent for acting without my approval!' the master knelt down and held out the edge of his robes as a sign of submission. The king continued in his display of authority: 'You are ordered to ensure that the brother Hugo of Jouy, who made the deal with the Sultan, is immediately banished from the kingdom of Jerusalem!'

96

The orders had to be obeyed, and nobody could do anything to prevent the brother from being banished from the city."

The humiliation for the Temple was such that the master Rinaldo of Vichiers was immediately expelled from the Order. We have no record of the debates of the Templars on the matter, as they were made in secret and without written testimony. However, we can deduce from the facts we do possess that a few weeks later Tomas Berard was named successor.

As far as Hugo of Jouy was concerned, it is known that he reached Spain, where he was named master of Catalonia. After a time he was confronted by several priests of the Order, and was obliged to request a bull from the Pope to enable him to deal with the rebels. The fact that the Pope acted in his favour shows that the events of the Holy Land had not affected his name too badly. Nothing more of him is known until his death in 1256.

CHAPTER XI

WHAT WAS HAPPENING IN EUROPE?

Despite everything, things keep growing

The internal fighting of the never-ending Reconquest in Spain, which more and more foreign forces were joining and other conflicts had not impeded the economic and demographic expansion in Europe. "Despite everything, things keep growing" was the phrase most frequently uttered by the European leaders.

It may be that one of the fundamental factors for such rapid development came from the monarchs' ever increasing predominance over the nobility. Power had been left in the hands of a person who represented a country instead of entrusting it to the many noble families who were often obliged to accord complicated pacts amongst themselves that more often than not ended up sparking off local wars.

Another example of progress can be seen in the foundation of universities such as those in Bologna, Paris, Montpellier, and Salamanca. This move succeeded in bringing culture out of the monasteries, though the majority of the professors were obliged to maintain their religious dedication. The official language throughout Europe was Latin, seen as a way of overcoming the kind of Tower of Babel that was needed in order to understand and communicate between each population and the dozens of dialects that existed within one nation.

Just as Latin was used as a unifying language, the paths of communication were opened, when the people started to understand the need for commercial exchange, something that was achieved with the pilgrimage routes to Santiago of Compostela, Rome and the Holy Land. The Venetians and the Genevans had widened the maritime routes for the transport of products to more isolated destinations, as had the textile industries of Flanders and other cities that manufactured metals or made wines and various quality products.

This new movement of people led to new knowledge of foreign cultures and religions. The information that had previously been brought by soldiers returning from battle, or the troubadours, who mixed imagination with reality, was now much more varied and authentic. When the first fairs appeared in different regions of France, the means of communication had to adapt to the new requirements. A type of currency was invented, which was widely recognised and understood, so that traders who moved large amounts of goods no longer faced the threat of being robbed on the roads, for robbers operated on almost every known route.

The national coins acquired unitary value, and began to be forged in gold, like the Tuscan florin. This move was attributed to the monarchs, who covered a larger area of territory and realised that it was easier to use coins than continue the exchange of goods.

The importance of the economic factor

With the considerable developments in commerce and industry, the concentration of capitals became more and more evident. Due to the long distances that had to be covered, it was no longer profitable to travel around to buy only small quantities. The Genevan and Venetian traders had shown that it was possible to transport large loads of cloth and other materials by sea, protected by the galleys from the risk of being robbed by pirates.

But more efficient protection was gained when the first banks were initiated, most of which focused on the clients that had come from the Templars and other military Orders. Deposited money was absolutely guaranteed not to be lost, and more importantly, a letter of credit could be used to extract the entire sum entrusted, minus a small charge of interest, many miles away or in a different country from where the original deposit had been made.

European cities also started to grow, due to the family management of large industries, such as that of textiles in Flanders. All these families were interdependent, which meant that they had to live close to each other, and in this way cities of more than thirty thousand inhabitants were born, which in turn required social, administrative and economic systems.

With the appearance of corporations and guilds, the most powerful patrons, the bourgeoisie, realised that they were in the hands of the merchants, who sold their products and made a profit, which usually tripled the amount paid.

The fact that this abuse was universally present in trade, and had been so since the beginning of time, did not convince the small producers. It had always been known that traders bought as cheaply as possible and sold the goods for much higher prices, but the action of several banks of not buying goods for a certain amount of time to force the producers almost to 'regulate' the fruits of their labour, led to the first known strikes in Flanders in about 1250.

The Church was always alert

The economic development led to the understanding that the common good, such as justice and social services, had to be under the control of a central power, and not managed according to the whims of different feudal lords. These services were therefore transferred to the monarchies. The historian Jaime Vignate wrote about these events in his work *The Enigma of the Templars:*

"In France, the process of national organisation came about quite quickly. In the case of Germany, the Polish duke of Merzovia summoned the Teutonic knights, who initiated from the lower Vistula the slow conquest of Prussia. They united German, Bohemian and Polish princes and knights in crusades, and between 1230 and 1350 the origins of a great warrior and monastic state were created. In England the matter was more complicated, as the monarchy was surrounded y a large number of small feudal governments according to Norman tradition, though it was mostly strong enough to impede the formation of compact feudal principalities, excepting those in the military confines of the North and West. In Spain the process was slower, due to the extent of power held by the regional authorities.

"The cultural concentration in the universities also created and developed particular tools, such as encyclopaedias and summaries. These represented the first developments of systematisation and method, a science understood as a different cultural instrument that went against dogma.

"The Church, very wary of losing control in the face of this rapid change, reacted strongly in all fields, excommunicating monarchs, forbidding loans with interest, and creating in 1231 the Inquisition, though the original idea of burning heretics can be attributed to Federico II (who was excommunicated)."

Gothic was not just an artistic genre

The gothic style arrived in Spain in 1140, when Abbot Sugar, who was chancellor of France and the Prince Regent for Louis VII while he was on the First Crusade, approved the plans for the Abbey of Saint Denis, including the first signs of gothic design on one of the choirs in the form of ogival arches and domes, flying buttresses, and other novel forms of architectural design.

The gothic style was slow to spread, but when it did it

magnified everything that the Middle Ages had represented. Landscapes filled their highest points with tall, thin cathedral spires, which did not need thick walls to support them. This beauty arrived first in French cities, then reached Belgium, Holland, England and Spain.

Strangely, Italy resisted this invasion of grandeur, content with the Roman style, which was closer to its San Francesco of Asis.

Louis Charpentier, the mythical Fulcanelli, explains a little more about the gothic style:

"The gothic dome is the result of an elastic arrangement of stone, created in such a way that the weight is projected upward instead of on the walls below. The walls' importance therefore became relative, for they could remain hollow or hold large glass images.

"The gothic was a totally original and unprecedented style, as the gothic dome is supported by two flying buttresses. The resulting squeeze effect means that the dome would break apart if the weight support of the key point of the dome was lost.

"The weight of those flying buttresses is what creates the pressure from the sides, and the weight of the stone dome itself is what causes the vertical pressure, always from the bottom to the top, on the point of the dome. The weight of the stone projects the dome upwards.

"The ogival cross, a classic gothic form, is made up of an arrangement of knots of tension, supported by the flying buttresses, which in turn rest on their buttresses, blocked by the weight of the pinnacles.

"The tensions produced are of such proportions that the labourers who worked for Viollet le Duc, one of the main cathedral constructors, were terrified by the fact that the smallest blow to some of the stones would create sound waves very similar to a tension spring or the strings of a giant musical instrument.

"Here, in the vibration that may or may not be audible, but always present in gothic buildings, is where the most efficient element of action on the people can be located, to whom the churches and cathedrals are dedicated, not only as cultural sites but also as a sort of common meeting place. A place which can also be used for dancing, as occurred on occasions in Chartres over the Easter period when the night watch was carried out by bishop himself. Ancient peoples also danced in the holy buildings on the most important dates of the year.

"In general, it is recognised that the gothic style came from the Cistercian Order, though according to Pierre du Columbire, the order served only as the commercial transporter of the style.

"The Order of the Temple is closely linked to the gothic style, via Saint Bernard, who brought education and mission to the Temple.

"Daniel Rops, who followed the criteria of Anne-Maria Armand, wrote: 'Several of the most singular characteristics of gothic architecture have their origins in Saint Bernard'. The Sons of Solomon were also intimately related to the Templars of Solomon, as is reflected in their name.

"A financer was required for the cathedrals. Only one man held the post, but with so many properties, he was in control of huge amounts of money. The Order of the Temple had its own enormous wealth, directed by wise chiefs.

"It is doubtful that the Temple would have taken on this role had they not been entrusted with it from the very beginning, because they were taught to act responsibly, and above all to respect the instigator of a work.

"The origins of so many enigmas were concentrated in Saint Bernard, who was responsible for the teaching and mission assumed by the Temple. In fact there were three missions. First was the search for the arc of Moses; secondly, the promotion of the development of western civilisation; and thirdly, the construction of the Temple of Christianity.

"The extraordinary thing is that the Templars did not falter for a moment from this mission. The records that we have of the commands show that the Temples provided defence, accommodation and food for the operators of the cathedrals. There has never been anybody that dared to doubt their prestige as hosts, defenders and providers. Nor was their merits as knights ever questioned, and even though the phrase 'to blaspheme like a Templar' was very common, and well-deserved, amongst the people of that age, this was only ever considered a venial sin."

Chapter XII

THE SLOW PATH TO DESPERATION

The tangle of minor conflicts

Louis IX of France left the Holy Land in 1254, once all the castles were in the hands of the military orders and almost all the Christian cities had been fortified. However, the minor conflicts continued to bristle, and in the long run would be damaging, for they never permitted the forces to concentrate on more important matters.

The election of the king of Jerusalem divided the Christian forces into three groups, who plotted in the shadows against the rest. The first choice for queen was the daughter of Isabel of Jerusalem and Henri of Champagne, Adela of Cyprus; then Hugo of Cyprus was selected, and a short time later the favourite was Conrad, the grandson of Friedrich II.

The diplomatic Tomas of Berard, who was the nineteenth master of the Temple, tried to remain uninvolved in the dispute, and when the conflict between the Venetian and Genevan traders arose, he took refuge in the Templar House of Saint Lazarus in order to avoid the arguments of both sides, for they took their dispute to Palestine. Unfortunately for him, the Venetians sought him out, and he was unable to refuse an interview with the count of Jaffa, the counsel of Pisa and the *bailio* of Italy, who managed to persuade him to send Temple knights to defend the town of San Juan of Acre. Tomas Berard completed the mission efficiently, but in the process some Genevans were killed when they tried to take over a number of houses, and he was accused of corruption and being bought by the Venetian merchants.

The Order reaction was to close ranks, as it constituted 'an absolute reign within another reign that was entrapped in the web of minor problems' this strategy gave the desired result, at least for a few years.

The menace of the Mongols to the Holy Land

In 1256, the Templars denounced the presence of the Mongolian armies, as they had invaded Armenia and left its cities in devastation. But they were largely ignored, as the victim was a Muslim country. In 1260 they again asked for assistance when they heard that the threat had moved to Syria, for they were very close to the Christian city of San Juan of Acre.

The master Tomas Berard wrote an infinite number of letters to the European leaders, one of which said the following:

"The Mongols march their prisoners at the rear of their troops, with the criminal result that they form a defensive barrier. Such savage action is causing a great number of innocent people to be killed."

He also described how the Mongols handled their bows, for they fired both forward and behind them whilst riding at great speed. He also underlined that the troops included women, who attacked as cruelly as the men.

It is likely that all Christianity breathed a sigh of relief when they heard that on invading Egypt, the Mongols had been defeated by the Emir Beybard, a reaction that was founded in the many years that the forces responsible for the failure of two crusades had not launched any attack on the Holy Land. It was mistakenly believed that the Mongol ex-slave was content with his rule over all of Egypt and other African countries.

Funds become scarce

The humiliation brought on the Templars by Louis IX had done nothing to damage the order's significance, as is demonstrated by the fact that in 1263, they asked the Pope to select brother Amalrico of Roche as treasurer of the royal finances of France.

With this course of action the holy king gave the impression that he considered the Temple as a sovereign state, whom he refused to offend by directly nominating the brother. As is logical, he was heard favourably, and Amalrico of Roche became master of the Temple of Paris. Some of the requests received during that period, such as those sent by the patriarch Guillerme II of Jerusalem, suggest that the Temple was experiencing a shortage of money.

The costs of maintaining the troops, supplying the castles and fortresses, and a thousand other economic obligations prevented the Orders from receiving large sums. Perhaps a Europe that was feeling less pressure from the Church than in previous ages was starting to forget the Holy Land.

The only order that continued to have comfortable economic funds available was the Templars, and they provided emergency loans for those who requested them, though they never forgot their status as a deposit for money that was entrusted to their hands to generate profits. This shows that they were not prepared to give up their position as bankers, and they offered aid only when they were sure of recovering the loan without excessive delay and with the corresponding interest.

The Mongol was the most feared threat

A clumsy political move on the part of the Templars and the Hospitallers, when they refused to execute an exchange of prisoners, led to the Mongol invasion of the Holy Land, something that had always been the principal underlying threat to the Holy Land. Once the Mongol troops had pillaged Nazareth and destroyed the church of the Virgin Mary, they attacked San Juan of Acre in 1263. They had insufficient forces to hold a prolonged siege though, and the attack on the city was limited to several raids.

At the beginning of 1264, the orders of the Templars and the Hospitallers united their forces in the conquest of the fortress of Lizon. The task was executed with relative ease, and victorious, the troops headed for Escalon. Meanwhile, the triumphs had motivated the French army, financed still by Louis IX, to approach the city of Beisan.

The reply from the Mongols was to attack the French territory of Carmel, and was successful in forcing all the Christians out. Then, unexpectedly, he retreated to Egypt, where it is known that he spent the month of January hunting. This news reassured the Christian forces, and for this reason Cesarea was materially defenceless when it was attacked by the Egyptian armies.

The Emir Berbers planned war with the cunning of a chess player. He needed only one week to destroy the city, though the survivors were allowed to escape. He did not show the same pity to the prisoners taken in Haifa, who were all executed.

In March, the conflict moved to the Hospitaller fortress of Arsuf, defended by some two hundred and seventy knights. They fought bravely until the walls were destroyed under the attack of the Saracen catapults, battering rams and the flaming bombs.

The chief of the fortress was forced to surrender when he realised that half of his arches had been lost, though he first signed an agreement to ensure the survivors' freedom. However, the treaty was not respected, and over seventy Hospitallers were sold as slaves.

Beybers' Saracens continued the advance toward San Juan of Acre, meeting with strong defences, which made the Mongol chief finally decide to call off war operations and return to Egypt. But he was careful to leave enough forces to defend the cities and fortresses that he had conquered. He was occupied with both internal and external matters, as he had just been named *Ikhan* of Azerbaijan, Mongol land in Asia.

The betrayal of a Temple brother

In 1268, the new invasion of the armies of Beybers had caused the loss of other important fortresses and cities, and the fortification of Gastein erected in the Orentes Valley found itself with the enemy only a few leagues away and short on provisions.Gastein was principally occupied by the Templars, whose repeated requests for assistance were ignored due to the need for aid in the places that were already under attack. Desperation must have been strong, and brother Guido of Belin succumbed to his fear.

While his companions were eating, and continually praying for help to arrive as soon as possible, the traitor escaped through a hidden door, taking with him the key to the main gate. He ran straight to the Sultan in charge of the Saracen troops, and handed him the key to the city.

The Saracens believed the brother, and sent only an emir and a patrol to take over the fortress. But as soon as they opened the gate, they were attacked by a shower of Christian arrows. Only a few managed to escape, including the Templar.

When they realised that they had been handed over to the enemy, the Templar knights escaped to Roca Guillaume, another fortress. There they were better able to organise their defences. They also sent word to San Juan of Acre of the dire situation they were in.

The master Tomas Berard had already received much bad news, but he started to organise Gastein's brother's salvation. He had no men to send as reinforcements, and was limited to sending the message that they held strong in Roca Guillaume. Then he and his men prayed, trusting in the God's will to save the unfortunate men.

His pleas were heard, but the matter of the abandonment of Gastein remained pending. Though the move had been forced by betrayal, it was totally prohibited by the rules of the Temple, and the survivors were put on trail. The proceedings took a long time, as all the masters of Europe were consulted, and after much deliberating the sentence of a year and a day without religious rights was decided, which was a minor penalty. The numerous judges took the fact that not a single piece of property had been harmed into account.

A scandal of conscience

After 1263, the situation of the Temple went through one of its worst times. In addition to Hugo of Jouy's actions, the order suffered a second scandal at the hands of Esteban of Sissey, the Major General of the Templars. Aside from legend, the reason for his excommunication is unknown. However, it must have been linked to him being relieved of his post. The proud Esteban refused to accept his punishment, and alleged that according to the rules of the order he could not be dismissed from his position unless the master himself ordered it. It seems that Tomas Berard must have given his support to the Major General, perhaps by feigning ignorance or recurring to stratagem, which was not uncommon in the clever master.

Thus Esteban of Sissey remained in hiding in Paris. He later moved to the south of France and then to Italy in an effort to avoid being found. When he heard of Urbano IV's death, he assumed that the new Pope would forget the situation, but when he discovered that Clement IV was acting with greater severity, he went to him on bended knee. His action freed him from excommunication, though he was gravely humiliated, and had to beg for forgiveness and promise that he would return to the Holy Land, where he would occupy the post of a simple foot soldier for a year.

According to the dark legend that weighed over the Templars, Esteban fled from an important battle when the life of his lover, a married lady from Beirut, was threatened. This action consisted of two sins: firstly abandoning a holy war, and secondly breaking his vow of chastity.

This version of events presents us with a dilemma: the support that Esteban received from the master Tomas Berard, which would imply that the conduct of the Templars had so degenerated that the breaking of sacred vows was tolerated.

It must be remembered that in the Middle Ages what was one day judged perverse could be holy the next. As proof of this in 1271, Esteban was made commander of Apulia, one of the most important places of the Temple. In this role he was able to accompany an important French nobleman to Palestine, where the once excommunicate gained a position in the entourage of the new Pope Gregory X. This series of events is difficult to explain from a modern perspective, in which past actions are remembered, but this was not the case in the Middle Ages.

The laments of a Temple troubadour

The European wars had led the Pope to ban the departure of crusades to the Holy Land, which had bloody consequences for the Templars and other Christians who were in dire need of human aid. Moreover, the economic aid was also being reduced. It is therefore not surprising that Oliviero, a Templar troubadour, wrote this literary lamentation:

"Rage and worry have taken control of my heart, to such extremes that I know not which force keeps me alive. All around me the cross is ill respected, the symbol that we converted into the standard as homage to He who died on the cross at the hands of infidels. The cross and its justice no longer have any value to us, for they no longer protect us, and have left us undefended before the cruel Turks, may God curse them for ever more! Though it is said, judging by recent events, that the Lord is determined that we remain here until our end arrives with no honour.

"We have watched powerless as they took Cesarea, and conquered the fortification of Arsur. May the Lord have mercy on us! To where did the sergeants and the rich merchants go who lived inside the walls of that place? We have lost so much land in Palestine that I have to admit we will never recover it.

"This should not make us think that the inhabitants of Syria feel pity. The same people that before welcomed us with cries of glory, have now sworn that they will not rest until no Christians remain in their lands. They are prepared to convert the monastery of Saint Mary into a mosque. For many of us, who should feel pained, appear to accept such sacrilege. Will this madness drive us to greet defeat with a smile, which we have become so accustomed to?

"I have to recognise that only a lunatic would dare to confront the Turks, for Jesus seems to take no side against them.

They have destroyed us, as they will continue to do from now on, which grieves me. French, Armenians, Persians and Tartars have all been destroyed, and the victors are safe in the knowledge that they will always defeat us, as our God, who previously remained alert, has abandoned us. It is Mohammed who has taken the reins, and who shines with power, and the cruel Sultan of Egypt shines too in his light.

"Now the Pope is magnanimous with the Provencal and French knights, who have joined his side in the fight against the Germans. He is showing great selfishness, in considering that the cross we defend here is inferior. He therefore wants everybody to forget the crusade so that nobody thinks any more about the battle that will be waged in Lombardy. I am wholeheartedly convinced that our legates would be capable of surrendering God and their indulgences for a bag of gold.

"French knights, recognise with me that Alexandria has caused you more pain than Lombardy. The Turks have taken your strength from you, and taken you hostage. They will never release you no matter the sum of the ransom, which always begging, you are prepared to pay!"

This text is a desperate cry, and proof that the Templars had lost all hope. Besieged by a bloodthirsty enemy that was growing stronger by the day, and hardly able to put up a defence, it is not surprising that they reacted in this way. Nor that they made some even more serious decisions.

Did they go as far as spitting on the cross?

This story is possibly no more than a rumour, though it would appear to be true. It is known that in 1267, the young Jacob of Molay, who was the last of the masters of the Temple, made the three vows that permitted him to enter the order. Present were Amalrico of Roche, as the master of France, and Umberto of Pairaud, as general inspector, as well as other knights.

After making his vows, the next Templar was draped with the white robe and placed before the cross, and then he was ordered to spit, an act that he had to refuse. But Jacob did spit, though on the floor.

This information is found in the confession made by Jacob to the court after the Inquisition had submitted him to mental and physical torture, with fasting and deprivation of freedom, and false promises. For this reason the information can be attributed to legend, to the lie that becomes truth once the speaker's will is defeated.

Another possibility considered by historians is that many details exist that support the story. The Templars had lost their faith in Jesus when the Pope and the other representatives of the Church abandoned them, and had denied him. The same applies to those who after having lost everything in the fight for Palestine found themselves facing a cruel death at the blade of the Saracens.

The true God, the saviour, was not with them then, for he had abandoned them to the mercy of a cruel end. Many died blaspheming, according to the survivors, so is it so strange that the Templars spat at the cross in their own form of blasphemy?

Chapter XIII

JERUSALEM HAS FALLEN!

The last master in the West

The master Tomas Berard died in 1273, and he was succeeded by Guillerme of Beaujeu, who had been Commander
of Apulia, and who bore the sad honour of being the last master in the West. He was born into nobility, a distant relative of
the king of France. He was a great traveller, diplomat and
man of culture.

There is a chance he attended the counsel of Lyon, in
which the Pope Gregory X spoke of the tragic situation in
Palestine. Christian properties in the land were now so scarce
that there had become almost testimonial, with the voracity of
the Emir Beybers, who had continued to conquer cities and
fortresses. However, his death in 1277 caused successive conflicts in Egypt, which allowed the Christians to recover
slightly. Problems related to dynasty also arose in the Christian territories, for sickness was indiscriminate of kings and
vassals. Politics led everybody to concentrate on the minor
problems that most affected the authorities, and the more
important matters were overlooked, as had happened since
the beginning of time.

It is also possible that the Palestinian nobility wanted to dazzle the rest of the people, in a demonstration of their importance. The courts of Cyprus, Tripoli and other cities were adorned such as London, Paris and Leon had never seen. Guillerme of Beaujeu remained at a discreet distance, for he had taken on enough responsibilities with the task of strengthening his Order. To this end he travelled to Spain, France and England, leaving the convents of the western Temple in good hands.

When he returned to the Holy Land, the war in Lombardy had forced many Genevans to seek refuge on the Syrian coast, where they also intended to confront the Venetians, still their sworn enemies. This rivalry between traders, however, did not stop them going about their business in Alexandria, business which was bringing deposits of great wealth to some of the Christian cities.

As had happened with other masters who had attempted to remain neutral, Guillerme of Beaujeu ended up being inclined toward the side of the Genevans. On many occasions he acted as mediator between the two enemies, usually in the ports after a battle. Thanks to his interventions many lives were saved, or at least, the prisoners were better treated.

The loss of Tripoli motivates the Christians

In March, 1287, the city of Tripoli was besieged by the troops of the Sultan Qelaun. Guillerme of Beaujeu had been aware of the threat for some weeks, due to his friendship with the Emir Salah. He tried to raise the alarm, but nobody took any notice. Only when the Saracens were a hundred leagues from the city was the threat recognised, and all ran to defend the walls.

Within the city were some of the best Knights of the Temple, the Hospitallers and the Teutonic Order. There were also high powered leaders, who tried to take command of the situation instead of giving it those who were accustomed to war. A second point against them was that the people had been celebrating a period of festivities, and were not in the best condition to go into war.

The walls were robust, but the Sultan must have had efficient spies, for he attacked at the only weak point. His great machines assaulted the spot until they managed to open a gap through which their well-armed cavalry could gain entrance. Added to this, their tallest towers had been destroyed, and Muslim arrows found an abundance of targets. The Christian soldiers only had to raise their heads above the ruins to meet their deaths by the enemy arrows.

The defeat was complete in the space of hours, and the Venetian and Pisan merchants fled from the city like rats deserting a ship. This provoked a great exodus of much of the surviving population, and the leader of the Hospitallers and a Major General of the Templars also fled, as two cowards who carried the noble charge of the knights of their Orders, who were left to fight until the last drop of their blood was spilt.

The loss of Tripoli resulted in the signing of a peace treaty, and also served to motivate the Pope and the European courts into action. They sent some twenty galleys full of crusaders, but they did not advise the commanders that they would be under leaders' orders in Palestine, nor that they must consult them, in their knowledge of the situation and of the terrain, before making any decisions.

An astute decision of the time

The crusaders installed themselves in San Juan of Acre, where many Muslims went in peace to buy goods or to sell their own products. There were also many Greek traders, most of whom wore beards, and who belonged to the Orthodox Church. These innocent traders may well have bore a slight resemblance to the Saracen soldiers, but only in physical appearance.

One day a group of recently arrived crusaders decided to clean the area around San Juan of Acre of its enemies, basing their judgement on nothing more than appearance, and the occasion ended in the murder of hundreds of innocent merchants, farmers and shepherds, who were not even carrying arms.

Sultan Qelaun's protests demanded that those responsible

were handed over, under threat of breaking the peace treaty. But there had been so many involved in the situation that the leaders resorted to a tactic that was typical of the period. Guillerme of Beaujeu's idea was to publicly execute the soldiers responsible, which would demonstrate that the crusaders had been responsible for the murder of the innocent Arabs. However, once again the master's advice was ignored. The city chiefs preferred to send their apologies to the Sultan, and await his reaction. But then fate intervened, with the death of Qelaun, which seemed to bring an end to the matter.

The siege of San Juan of Acre

But the new Sultan was not prepared to forget the events, and considered it so important that it was the prime matter that he wanted to resolve, though not by diplomatic means. He did, however, send word to the master of the Temple, which demonstrates the relations that existed between the Templars and the Muslims. His letter warned of the immediate attack of the city.

Guillerme of Beaujeu informed the city chiefs of what was about to happen, and on this occasion they did listen to him, and immediately sent emissaries to the Sultan bearing gifts and papers, to request a meeting to find a way of resolving the matter peacefully. The Sultan's response was to shut the emissaries in his dungeons, where they were left to die of starvation and thirst.

The siege of San Juan of Acre began at the beginning of April, 1288. Thousands of Muslim tents were set up around the city walls, and the Christians calculated that the enemy numbered some fifteen thousand soldiers, in contrast to their own seven hundred armed knights and forty thousand peaceful civilians, most of whom were women, children and the elderly.

The Marmeluke guard was replaced four times a day, and the Sultan's crimson tent, called a *dehliz*, was always open and mounted on a platform opposite the city's great gate, giving the idea that it would not be removed until San Juan of Acre was conquered.

Only heroism remained

It took the Muslims three days to set up their giant catapults, directed at the strongest towers of the city, and erected barriers out of tree trunks on the other side of the moat that surrounded the three city walls which did not face the port.

The Christian defences attempted to stop the barriers being raised, but the Arabs were protected by shields, and escaped with few injuries throughout the many hours of labour. Moreover, the catapults were launching great stones at the city, though the towers remained standing. In the afternoon, an imprudent chief opened the city gate and attacked the first line of Marmelukes, which introduced them to another terrible weapon of the enemy – the *carabaos*, black bulls, which were released amongst the terrible chaos and ran riot, trampling everything in their path. Many Christians met their deaths as a result, though the survivors were able to retreat inside the city and close the gate, thick enough to resist the assault of the enraged soldiers on the other side.

Some days later, the main defence tower of San Juan of Acre was destroyed, killing half a hundred occupants in the process. The task was achieved by the Arab sappers, who managed to undermine the tower's foundations, while the catapults pounded it from above. A huge gap was left in the wall from the tower falling, which had to be defended at all costs. The Christians blocked the hole with the ruins of the tower itself.

That night the Christians took advantage of the cease-fire initiated with the sunset, and ventured out of the city in an attempt to burn the enemy's wooden barriers. But the venture did not go according to plan. Some of those in charge of lighting the barrier were so scared that when they threw the lit torches, instead of hitting the tree trunks, they set light to the dry scrub and awoke the Muslims who were sleeping nearby. They were so confused, however, that the Christians were able to kill them easily. The rest of the huge camp appeared not to have realised what was happening, and as nobody challenged them, the patrol leaders decided to destroy some of the tents. They mounted their horses and advanced cautiously. But the fires had been extinguished, the night was black and they did not know the terrain, and the horses' legs got caught in the ropes of the tents. The horses started in fright and the soldiers were thrown noisily to the ground, and in minutes the surprise attack became a deadly trap. More than twenty Templars and Hospitallers were lost that night.

Despite this failure, the Christians continued making nightly patrols, most of which ended in the same way, for the Arabs kept watch in the shadows. When the Christians approached they lit their beacons, which startled the Christians into paralysis, and they were killed before they could even react. Perhaps their God still had no wish to protect his faithful soldiers.

Thus, the only remaining possibility open to the knights of San Juan of Acre was heroism, and survival instinct. Few wanted to surrender while they were still capable of fighting, and they still harboured the faint hope that if they could hold off the attack for long enough, reinforcements would arrive by sea, where the enemy were defenceless.

The sea gives hope and destroys it

In the first week of May, reinforcements arrived in the form of the king of Cyprus, and the besieged population was filled with hope. Now that the Christians had an army of over a thousand men, some of the leaders believed that they would be able to sign a treaty with the Sultan. But they were outnumbered by those who thought that such a gesture would be seen as cowardice by the Pope and the European courts, and it was decided to continue in the defence of the city.

While discussions were being held, another of the great towers was destroyed. The panic that took hold of the people was so great that thousands of them ran out to the Cypriot, prepared to offer all they had to gain passage out of the city. The ship captains may have accepted the proposal, but they could not confront the weather.

A terrible storm struck, filling the sky with forks of lightning and bellowing thunder, and raising huge waves forty feet high, leaving the people who had been so desperate to escape forced to seek refuge in what was still standing of their houses. Many died from the resulting panic, falling into the sea, trampled by others and in the crush to reach safety, and it is possible that more were killed from the general panic than from the Muslim attack itself.

The sea had brought hope to the people of San Juan of Acre, and destroyed it in one foul swoop. When the storm ended, the other threat appeared: the Arabs had demolished the last defences and gained entry to the city.

The courageous agony of the last master of the Temple

Guillerme of Beaujeu came out of his refuge when the Arab bugle sounded. He reached the door of Saint Anthony with ten of his knights, the master of the Hospitallers and other soldiers, all of whom were armed with their only remaining defence, heroism, for other weapons would do them little good now.

The fire launched continuously by the Muslims had started hundreds of fires, and dense smoke prevented anybody seeing more than two feet in front of them. Many Christians were confused with Arabs, and vice versa, in the hand to hand fighting that resumed. Suddenly an arrow struck the master of the Temple below the left shoulder, just where he was not protected by his armour. The point penetrated a hand's length into his chest, but the knight hardly felt the pain in the heat of the battle, and continued astride his horse. But the wound disoriented him and he guided his horse in a different direction from that of his companions. Somebody shouted to him:

"For God's sake, master, do not desert us, without you we will lose the city much more rapidly!"

And the brave soldier-monk answered, with his voice still strong, "My brothers, my strength fails me, I have been shot, see the wound!"

He pulled the arrow from his shoulder and threw it to the ground, nearly falling from his horse. The others ran to him, laid him on a large shield, and carried him to the palace of Maria of Antoquia. There he was treated and the armour cut from his shoulders. Then he was wrapped in a blanket and taken to the beach.

He could not be put onto a ship for the sea was still very rough, and they had to leave him in the Temple convent, still free from Muslims. Even in his death throes the master never stopped begging the men to sign a treaty with the Muslims, and he died with this request on his lips.

Does cruelty know no limits?

The Muslim troops conquered San Juan of Acre and annihilated all those who remained, irrespective of sex or age. In their frenzy of killing they wiped out everybody like death himself, with no regard for his victims.

Fortunately the Christians still had the tower of the Temple, whose walls were thick, and able to resist thousands of attacks. They were also protected on almost all sides by the sea, by which they had previously been able to save many innocent lives, once the sea had calmed and the ships could leave the port.

The remaining survivors, who numbered some two hundred, sought refuge in the tower of the Temple, under the command of Pedro of Sevry, who was an efficient administrator and chief. For ten endless days they managed to hold off the siege, hardly sleeping, and sharing the meagre rations between them.

Then the Sultan ordered a cease-fire, and on the next day he sent emissaries to inform the Christians that if they surrendered their lives would be pardoned. The Major General of the Temple had to accept, for they hardly had any provisions. But when he saw the Arabs' mistreatment of the women, he gave the order to expel the infidels, and all the Muslims were killed at the tower door.

The Sultan did give the order to resume the siege, but requested that they send negotiators, for he was prepared to sign a different agreement. Pedro of Sevry believed his words, and marched out with the group, but this was a terrible mistake. It seems impossible that the Major General could have been forgetting the murderous conduct of the Saracens.

124

Perhaps he thought that he would receive better treatment due to his status as a Christian Templar.

Pedro of Sevry and the other negotiators were executed as soon as the reached the Sultan's tent, and the executioners put their heads on spikes to show them to the occupants of the tower. They continued their resistance desperately, but their fate was now decided.

The tower began to tremble as though being shaken by an earthquake, for the Muslim sappers had once again undermined its foundations. Then the Christians did surrender, but the attackers stormed the tower while the prisoners were still inside, and the foundations were unable to bear the weight. The fall of stones and bricks not only crushed the three hundred people who were inside, but also more than two thousand Marmelukes that were gathered around it.

With the loss of San Juan of Acre there remained little to defend in the Holy Land. The new master of the Temple, Theobald Gaudin, left for Cyprus to request assistance, but everybody believed that life in the doomed Holy Land was no longer possible. Entire detachments preferred to desert, and most of the Christians escaped, in the face of certain death at the hands of a cruel enemy, leaving only the Templars with their Pilgrim Castle.

The knights that defended Beirut handed the keys of the city to a Turkish emir after a terrible siege, and once again the Saracens did not respect the agreement made and hanged all the Christians, in a show of limitless cruelty.

It seemed that the violence was indeed without bounds, and the enemies found themselves in a spiral of death and vengeance, which descended into an inferno of incredible proportions.

However, yet more terrible was the fact that the Pope and the European courts did not act. Whereas previously the reaction had been the immediate organisation of crusades, on this occasion nothing was done, and the reason for this can be found in one of the most fantastic farces in the history of humanity, concerning the last master of the Temple, that was mounted in Paris.

Chapter XIV

NEVER GIVE REFUGE TO A HYENA

The fragile power of the Parisian Templars

As many historians have verified, the three religious orders that fled from Palestine had very different runs of fortune. The Hospitallers easily found a place in Cyprus, where they ended up becoming a maritime power that competed with the Genevans and Venetians. The Teutonic order returned to Germany, where they had a seat and continued to prosper. But what happened to the monks from the powerful Order of the Temple?

First they went to Cyprus, where the Hospitallers had already established themselves. But they were not satisfied, and soon moved on to France, overlooking the fact that there, as in Spain and in England, their previous situation had been much better, and the brothers there enjoyed great prestige, as well as much property and wealth.

The Templars went to Paris, as they possessed there a large heritage and some valuable buildings, and above all because they had always considered themselves French, owing to the founders of the Order and the nationality of most of their members.

This sentimental error of putting the love of the homeland before material and religious interests also distracted them from the fact that their Parisian bank was not in the good state as it had been. Due to manipulation on behalf of Philippe IV's counsellors, the government of the ancient institution no longer corresponded entirely to the Temple, and now found itself under the control of the monarch's whims. This weakness seems obvious to us today, but perhaps in those times was almost impossible to detect. The monks of the Temple still considered themselves very powerful, as the words of the great historian Michelet demonstrate:

"They arrived in France as the bearers of an immense fortune, made up of one hundred and fifty thousand gold florins and ten mules laden with silver. What did they intend in times of peace with such forces and riches? Were they perhaps considering the possibility of establishing sovereignty in the West as the Teutonic knights had in Prussia and the Hospitallers in the Mediterranean islands? There was no other country where they could count a higher number of secured places, nor where they were so strongly linked to the nobility."

It is certain that all the treasure of the French crown was under the management of the Templar bankers, as well as further riches that tripled the royal treasury in quantity. The situation appeared, from the outside, to be the same as ever, and provided them with a sense of security for the future.

A second circumstance that went towards creating a sense of security amongst Jacob of Molay and his men was that they considered themselves superior, and able to easily resolve any problem. Perhaps they felt protected by a higher power, which was related neither to worldly powers nor those traditionally preached by the church. Here we face another enigma, which we will explore further later on.

A greedy and manipulated king

Philippe IV was crowned in 1285. He was blond, tall

and well proportioned, and soon became known for his looks. But what few people knew was that he had not been an able student, except in his lessons with figures; that he had a poor control of discourse and was forced to learn his speeches, all very brief, beforehand; and that his mind was slow to find answers and replies. However, he did quickly learn his limitations.

Despite these faults, he felt so strongly drawn to money that he would do almost anything to obtain more. As a young child he had learnt that if he wanted a full purse he had to entrust himself to his servants, in particular to those who shared his quality of ambitiousness. Various mistakes in this field led him to deduce that his advisers should neither be mean nor conceited; rather they should advance their fortunes without making enemies along the way.

As with anybody who is aware of their weakness but able to conceal them, he exchanged his faithful servants for advisers who desired wealthy futures, and who assumed that the protection of a monarch, whose benefit must always be priority, would also ensure benefits for them. The king thus put himself in the hands of Guillerme of Nogaret.

Guillerme of Nogaret, the jackal

The son of a bourgeois family, Guillerme of Nogaret studied law. He was named judge at only twenty years of age, and this made him so famous that he was summoned to Paris, where he soon became part of the king's court. He was made a knight, and later named ambassador in Rome. There he crossed Pope Boniface VIII's path, who reprimanded him with insulting words that were to remain in his spiteful thoughts forever. He never forgave the Pope, and consequently came to consider him one of his most hated enemies.

On his return to Paris he continued his activities as a judge, and soon found the way to preside over the most important trials, regardless of the social or religious status of the accused parties. In this way he arranged for the trial of Bernard of Saisset, the bishop of Pamiers accused of blasphemy, heresy and other similar crimes, with the aim of condemning him. However, he was unable to dictate the sentence he had in mind, due to the intervention of important witnesses, and the experience led him to aim much higher.

Guillerme of Nogaret was the friend of the Pope's worst rivals, and found a legitimate way to avenge himself for the harsh words and humiliation that he had suffered in his time as ambassador in Rome. Taking his time, manipulating powerful influences and travelling from one side of Europe to the other, he managed to physically place Boniface VII in the accused bench. To achieve this he had to create a council, before which he made the charges of sodomy, theft from the church, abuse of power leading to the death of thousands of innocents, despotism, conspiracy with infidels, the obtaining of personal wealth at the cost of the Church, and heresy.

But dethroning the Pope turned out to be more complicated than Guillerme had thought. When he discovered that all his attacks could be turned against him, and worse, against the king of France, he formed a plot with Boniface IV's fiercest rivals. The result was the assassination of the Pope at Anagni.

The following Pope, Benedict XI, started to work on Guillerme Nogaret's excommunication, but he died on the day before he was due to dictate the sentence. It took almost a year to elect the new Pope, who was Beltran of Got, the archbishop of Bordeaux. The new Pope had already forgotten the matter, as it was due to the pressures of the king that he had been elected.

Guillerme had won, and he wrote a letter to the king straight away, offering his services. He therefore became the king's favourite, and the principal adviser for a monarch who required others to do his thinking for him. As far as the financial situation was concerned, the king had made a good choice, but as for moral and human issues, it was another matter: the king was to find himself at the mercy of an abominable man, who knew no limits when it came to fulfilling his ambitions, as we can see from his destruction of the Pope, who had been the highest power in European Christianity, and therefore in the whole world.

The propitiatory victim

Jacob of Molay was born in 1244, near Besançon. He took his Templar vows at twenty-one, and went straight to the Holy Land, where he was under command of Guillerme of Beaujeu. He was chosen as the master of the order in 1294. He was very concerned with military affairs, and his only wish was to return to Palestine, where he would be able to regain all the power that had previously belonged to the order.

His mission took him to Bordeaux, where he would set about presenting his plans to the Pope Clemente V. He had considered every aspect of his visit, excepting one very important fact: he was about to face a pawn of the king, a person so weak that he would be capable of sacrificing thousands of lives for fear of offending the one who had seated him in Peter's Seat. We only need to analyse the reasons that he invented for moving to Bordeaux, together with the fact that most of the cardinals around him were French, to see that he was entirely dependent on the king of France's will. However, Jacob of Molay was unaware of this.

The Pope did hear him attentively, and even gave him several bulls to set up Templar chaplains once again in the Palestine, in addition to other benefits that they had previously possessed. He was full of good words, administrative gestures and smiles, but nothing more.

With Jacob of Molay being the propitiatory victim, whom he could force to wait as long as necessary and the fact that he knew that he would never raise his voice in protest... could it just be that this weak man acted on more ulterior motives? We will address this question further on, when we come to explore the secret missions and the great accomplishments of the Templars.

The jackal joins forces with the vulture

In 1306, Guillerme of Nogaret was as active as ever. He had one of the greatest abilities in France to shred the most absolute truths leaving only a pile of doubts, an incredible skill with words and verbal reflexes that confused anyone who stood against him. And he never stopped searching for allies of his own level.

For this reason he took pains to seek out the inquisition General Guillerme of Paris, taking advantage of the fact that he had just been named as personal confessor to King Philippe. He had already filled this position and that of tutor to the king's children. Only one or two private conversations between the men were enough to determine that they had a common enemy – the Order of the Temple.

The inquisitor hated the Templars for the immense power that they had accumulated, while the king's principal adviser hated them for their wealth. Two motives that could be separated or joined, as riches and power go together. Thus the jackal and the vulture understood that from that point on they should launch a united attack. However, they needed the king of France behind them, and Guillerme of Nogaret took charge of this task.

When greed takes over

The greedy king of France was involved in many political projects, for he wanted to extend the power of France to the North and East. The expensive gifts made to important collaborators, related to the maintenance of his own court, had almost ruined him. As the king had complained to him on several occasions of the situation, Guillerme of Nogaret reminded him of the quickest way to refill the royal strong rooms: to seize the wealth of all the Jews that lived in France, just as had been done with the Lombard people in the past.

The monarch approved the proposal without having to consult his other advisers, for he remembered the success of the first great confiscation. The most surprising thing of this huge robbery was not the quantity seized, but in the stealth of the royal officials who had executed the exercise. We must assume they were either very well paid or that they were promised a share of the profits, as not one of them warned the Jews of the forthcoming crime.

Guillerme himself directed the most important seizures, and a month later he presented his king with a caravan of wagons, filled with money, jewels and valuable objects. They gathered so much gold that Philippe IV decided to mint a new coin, in order to regulate the money that circulated within the country. But on this occasion his greed pushed him too far, and the population of Paris rioted against him. He was forced to seek refuge in the castles of the Templars. And Jacob of Molay himself took him to the most comfortable quarters, ignorant of the imprudence of offering refuge to a hyena, especially when the first thing he asks is to see the treasures in the strong room. The request was thought unusual, but no attempt was made to prevent it, and once in the darkness of the huge cellars the expression of greed on the king's face was not distinguishable.

The problems with the rebels were soon resolved, as Guillerme mobilised the royal guards, who arrested the leaders of the outbreak. They were brought to justice, and the entire country was forced to accept the new coinage, even though they lost out in the change. Thus their king's greed was satisfied, though only temporarily, for greed is a sickness that will not rest even with all the riches of the world.

A repeated lie can become a truth

The lie was born in 1303, when one of the first to hear it was Jaime I of Aragon in the city of Lerida, from the lips of Esquius of Floyrac:

"You should know, most holy lord, that the Templars refuse God in their oath of initiation, and moreover they prostrate themselves before an idol in the form of the devil."

But the Spanish king did not take the news seriously, and dismissed the messenger with no further thought. It is known that the bearer of the lie was a Templar who had been expelled from the Order, though it is not known why. In his quest for revenge he visited countless nobles, rich bourgeoisie and bishops, in a long pilgrimage that took him to Paris in 1307. Once again he spread his lies, this time attracting the attention of Guillerme of Nogaret, who realised how the lie could be manipulated into an unquestionable truth.

He gave money to Esquius, after advising him not to mention their meeting to anybody, and went into action. He went straight to Guillerme of Paris, who granted him a list of all the commanders and nobles who had heard similar stories in the Holy Land.

The royal adviser spoke to several of these people, and once he judged that he had gathered enough evidence, which should never have been considered incriminating by somebody with his legal experience, he took the matter to the king.

Perhaps he made a proposal similar to that which had allowed the confiscation of all the wealth of the Lombards, and later of the Jews. We do know that Philippe IV informed Pope Clemente V in the first interview they maintained. As the matter in hand was deeply serious, he was advised to make his accusations formal, which would officially open the case.

The master Jacob of Molay heard the accusations and called a meeting of the most important knight of the Order. Some had been able to talk with the Pope, who had said that he considered the accusations so unbelievable that he was not prepared to give them even a moment of his attention. This made the order feel secure, and as they separated they were laughing as though nothing had occurred. For how could they have known the moral depravity of their enemy? They could never have realised that Philippe IV's main adviser had previously accused a bishop, and later the Pope himself, of heresy, nor that they were now being accused of similar sins themselves.

But other questions should also be addressed, regarding the actions of Jacob of Molay and the other Templars.

In August, the Pope informed the king that an investigation into the Order of the Temple had been ordered, for which all the evidence that had been gathered would be required. However, he also advised that he needed to undertake certain medical care, and that the case must therefore be delayed until October.

Guillerme of Nogaret was not prepared to wait that long. He had drawn up all the accusations and sent them secretly to the inquisitors most closely linked to the king of France. They were silently awaiting the order to act.

The accusations made against the Temple

The historian Fulcanelli, or Louis Charpentier, recorded the accusations made against the Templars:

"With the aim of defeating the Temple through its most important knights, the inquisitors were given a questionnaire, which was then to be passed to the courts. The document has been preserved until the present day. The accusations it contains can be summarised in the following way:

1. Novices had to wear a blindfold when all deposits were made. All actions were shrouded in secrecy, and carried out at the time when all other members were sleeping or under cover of darkness.

2. Novices were always forced to refuse Jesus, the cross, God and the Virgin Mary, as well as all the holy saints. This was an essential initiation requirement to enter the order.

3. Novices were told that Jesus had never been the authentic God, and that his mission on Earth was only that of a prophet. The motive of his crucifixion was not to save human kind, but as the best form of punishment for the serious crimes he committed during his life.

4. Novices were forced to spit on the cross, and in later instruction were taught never to believe in the sacraments of the altar, nor those that the church upheld.

5. All the Templars believed that only their own great master could absolve them of their sins. Pardon was sometimes granted by some of the Temple professors or inspectors, regardless of the fact that they may be laymen.

6. The priests of the Temple intentionally forgot the sacred words of the consecration during mass.

7. One of the first things recommended to novices was not to resist carnal union with other members of the Order.

8. Once the period of initiation was over, the novice and the brothers who had accompanied him kissed each other on the mouth, on the belly button and on the naked stomach. On occasions they also kissed the anus, the bottom of the spine, the buttocks and the inside of the thighs.

9. All areas of the Temple possess idols, in the form of particular heads. Some of these have three faces, others only one, and others the shape of a skull. The Templars affirm that internal salvation can be reached through these heads, and if they pray to them they will grant great wealth, cause barren trees to bear blossom, and unploughed soil to germinate wheat.

10. The Templars generally tied these heads to their bodies with ropes, concealed beneath their robes and in permanent contact with the skin. They were taught be their tutors to carry them always, even when they slept at night."

To these accusations were added some brief complementary questions:

1. Did all the above take place with which the accused is familiar?

2. Do you believe that they were practised in all kingdoms and other places?

3. Were such practices carried out by all the members of the Order, by only a certain few, or was it a practice made in view of others?

4. Was it an ancient ritual?

5. Did these customs form part of the rules of the Order?

6. Was the totality of these practices, uses, duties and instructions included in the rules of the Order after the Pope had authorised the original rules?"

Were these soldier-monks heretics?

On 12th October, 1307, after a week of intense rain, the

city of Paris awoke to a clear sky. It could be said that even the sky wanted to witness the great event that the day brought: the burial of Catherine of Couternay, wife of Charles of Valois and daughter of Philippe IV, and a beautiful woman who had been loved by her people. The ceremony was attended by all the most important people of France, including Jacob of Molay, who wore a black sash and marched beside the king. It is difficult to believe that the soldier-monk was suspected of such terrible crimes.

On the following day the royal guard, the lords of justice and other forces went into action with surprising efficiency. Most of them had had experience with the Lombards and the Jews, and in this case the enemy were fewer, though more powerful.

None of the Temple building had closed their doors, and many victims were surprised whilst going about their everyday routines, about to go out or asleep. Only a few saw the patrols and, foreseeing the coming events, hanged themselves or threw themselves out of a window.

The Templars possessed over two thousand estates, including castles, churches and other properties, and the operation must have included more than five thousand agents, who covered the whole of France. Events were competed with impressive synchronisation within two days, and constituted one of the extraordinary human raids carried out during the Middle Ages. In those times leaders dictated detention orders that covered entire empires.

Once again it is difficult to understand how not a single Templar realised the danger that was forthcoming. We could consider that some information was leaked to those who managed to take their own lives before they were arrested. However, they did not flee on hearing the news, only on seeing the patrols did they realise the threat was true and take such drastic action.

And considering the manner in which monks trained for fighting allowed themselves to be imprisoned, is it possible that they were all heretics? It is possible that at some point in their history they had been.

Legends tend to originate with isolated occurrences, which are later assembled to compose a dramatic series of events. Perhaps heretic actions were witnessed in some Temple seats, just as there had been occasional traitors and deserters among them. All societies, especially those with a history of over two hundred years, have exceptions to the rule.

In the case of Jacob of Molay and his men, we can also bear in mind the idea of reincarnation, or the belief that beyond death there existed a heavenly life that they had earned. The highest powers of the Temple at least must have believed this, although we will see that fewer of the inferior brothers must have had such faith, by the manner in which they defended their lives.

The other enigmas were to have their origins in the atrocities that we are about to discover in the following chapters.

CHAPTER XV

AN EXTRAORDINARY FARCE

The treasure of the Temple of Paris

Guillerme of Nogaret, the jackal who acted as judge and adviser of King Philippe, made the arrest of Jacob of Molay personally. He arrived accompanied by two royal guards, who carried poisoned swords. There was no need for him to read the accusations, for his expression of triumph and scorn revealed all.

That afternoon, the King of France had had free run of the Templar castle, where he had entered the cellars not as a guest, but as the owner. He was not disposed to await the judges' decision, for he knew that in reality the decision was already certain, and gave the order that the riches, which tripled those of the royal treasury (also deposited with the Temple) were to be moved to a new place, for which only he had the key.

However, even this did not sate his greed, for he still awaited all the money of which he had taken possession from the different Templars of France. It would not be as much as the quantity he had just received, thanks to the cunning of his favourite adviser, but it would include hundreds more stores filled with gold coins and valuable objects.

Thousands of confessions forced by torture

All the interrogations were handled by Guillerme of Paris, the great inquisitor, the vulture. Just as his colleague had expertly organised the royal guard in the arrest operation, he took care to send the accusations to all the inquisition judges of the kingdom, accompanied by an emphatic order:

"These children of the devil will refuse to confess their sins, for they are so grave that they will be unable to speak them. You must force them by the methods that you know, as only physical weakness will succeed in loosening the tongues of the enemies of the church, as we have seen in the past."

Thus the torture chambers were put into action, and the Templars subjected to the most horrible suffering: broken bones, red-hot irons, pliers that tore skin and flesh, lit brasses and other merciless tactics, which forced even the strongest to deny his firmest beliefs, for the pain became unbearable, and when it did not bring death it took its victims, already weakened by injustice and the sense of powerlessness, to madness. We can then add the lack food and water, sleep depravation, the condition of the cells and the brutal treatment of the jailers, and it is no surprise that the result was thousands of confessions.

Some of the confessions

We turn once more to Louis Charpentier to examine some of the confessions forced from the Templars:

"Jacob of Molay, the great master (who was never subjected to torture):

"Brother Humbert brought a bronze cross bearing the image of Christ, and invited me to deny him. I had to obey because he obliged me by force."

Hugo of Payraud, the inspector of France:

140

"Afterward brother Jean showed me a cross bearing the image of Christ. He forced me to deny the figure that was before my eyes, and then spit on the cross. I admit that I obeyed, but only with my lips, and never with my senses and my heart."

Godfrey of Charnay, tutor of Normandy:

"As soon as they informed me that I had just entered the Order and placed the cape on my shoulders, they brought me a cross with the figure of Jesus, and brother Amaury (prior of France and personal friend of Saint Louis) told me never to believe in the figure before me, for he had only come to Earth to fulfil a mission as a false prophet, and that I should therefore never consider him my God. Then he forced me to deny Christ on three occasions."

Godfrey of Gonneville, tutor of Aquitania and of Poitou:

"Brother Robert (of Torteville, the master of England) held an open missal before me, on the page where a cross and the image of Jesus appeared. He threatened that I would lose everything if I did not deny the Jesus that was put in the cross. I exclaimed, 'But lord, how can you ask me to do such a thing? I will never obey!' and he replied, 'you only have to do it without thinking. I swear to you on the eternal salvation of my soul that you will not regret what I ask you to do, nor will you ever feel remorse or conscience.'

Reinold of Tremelay, prior of the Temple of Paris:

"As soon as I entered I had to deny Christ."

"And the Templars also confessed to the charges of forcing novices to deny Christ and the cross as they were initiated into the Order."

Strangely, most of these confessions were obtained without physical torture, for even Guillerme of Paris did not dare to go so far with such important people. We do know that he promised to spare their lives, return them a part of their wealth and continue noble, but non-religious activities in a distant place. These, however, turned out to be promises he never intended to keep, and which he used as bait, just as if they were helpless rabbits.

These events took place over a period of many months, and the high Templars were able to follow them from outside the prisons, where the people who were convinced by paid agitators demanded their heads. They were also able to read the confessions made by the inferior brothers with torture.

Faced with such pressure, they must have confessed to so many lies to conserve their freedom, for they firmly believed that as soon as they could enlist their friends' help that truth would be revealed. For surely the nobles who had visited the Holy Land or were long-time guests of the Templars in their residences in France would not believe the lies.

The soldier-monks of that time, who had fought along-side the Muslims and whose cruelty had sometimes been diabolical, seemed unaware that the enemy who worked in the shadows to manipulate the entire situation would leave no stone unturned. Each of the thousands of confessions was copied out a hundred times, with careful note of the confessor's personal details, and the copies were sent to the Pope and to councils all over Europe.

Some of the confessions obtained with torture

Here we can refer to the historian Alejandro Vignati, and his book *The Enigma of the Templars:*

"At this time we are facing one of the greatest mysteries of the Temple, and we will concentrate on he who caused a shudder of panic to so many nobles: the devil Baphomet.

"In the accusation acts, the name of an idol appears on numerous occasions, with the appearance of a human head with long beards, and which the Templars worshipped in their chapters. More specifically in the article: 'They prostrated themselves to worship an idol that they considered our God, the saviour who would bring them eternal rest. They believed that the head was able to protect them from all evil, that it would grant the Order vast riches, and that it had the power to make barren trees blossom and wheat sprout from the driest soil.' As can be understood, the Templars later started to confess to having been subjected to the most inhumane torture: brother Jean Taillefer, from the diocese of Langres, declared that as soon as he was initiated into the order he had been forced to prostrate himself before this Baphomet, who was on the centre of the altar. It was an idol of human appearance. Hugues of Bures, from Burgundy, said that he was shown a head that had been taken from a closet that served as a chapel. The head appeared to be made of different metals: copper, silver and gold. It had the appearance of a human man with a long beard, and could have been white.

"The Templar Rudolph of Gisi confessed that he attended a general chapter directed by the brother of Villers and given by the diocese of Troyes, during which brother Hugues of Besançon left the head of an idol on a wooden seat. The novice panicked so much that he escaped from the chapter without receiving absolution. Rudolph of Gisi, when interviewed for a second time, declared that he had seen a similar head in seven chapters. In accordance with his confessions we know that the idol had a horrible diabolical form. Each time that he was shown the head he felt such horror that he was paralysed and was too weak even to look at it.

"The confessions continue, giving us an idea of the horrible depths that human testimony can reach when burned by the horror of torture. There is no doubt that the brothers went beyond the intentions of the judges, maybe in the hope of arousing their pity. They told how they could hear how Baphomet spoke; how he foretold oracles, though they were unable to remember the contents of these, though the judges were satisfied with the information, and had obtained more evidence than they needed. On other occasions it was declared that the devil took the form of a black cat or a crow, and events ended up in a satanic rite. In these times, witches' Sabbaths were being celebrated, which required the appearance of many demons, apart from Baphomet, that took pleasure from the bodies of white and beautiful maidens, whose nakedness was only covered by their long black hair."

What was not revealed in the reports of the accusations was of vital importance: in none of the two thousand properties of the French Templars was any idol, or any head, found that could be attributed to Baphomet. Only one perfectly shaped head was found of a man covered with white hair, forged from silver and gold, and which in actual fact was no more than a relic.

The hyena, the jackal and the vulture complete a satisfactory mission

If we stop and examine the huge number of confessions, we can see that they lack any accusatory value. It is true that in the Middle Ages things were viewed differently, such as the custom of calling the confrontation between two knights a 'duel of God', in which the reason was granted to the winner, regardless of his state of ability, strength and condition at the time.

Many had already questioned the legality of the judges of the Inquisition, but if we consider that such methods continued to be used until the eighteenth century, with the exception of a few periods, we can understand what occurred in France during those years.

What makes the events most difficult to understand are the occurrences in other countries, where the Templars were also interrogated. In Spain, Italy, Portugal, Germany and Sicily, where the judges of the Inquisition did not employ methods of torture, they found nothing of what their French colleagues uncovered.

The foundations of this great farce and infamous monumental theatre can be found in the almost two hundred years of the Templars' existence. At the time of these judgements they numbered no more than fifteen thousand in all the West, compared with over half a million other monks of the Church. Only a tenth of them could read and write, for the majority were illiterate: lambs in a great flock that followed always the shepherd's steps.

The Templars not only were cultured, but they would also have been educated from their customary contact with other religions and forms of society. Among their customs were some influenced by the Muslims, such as the tendency to wash, trim or shave their beard, and even to wear perfume. All these habits went against their traditional ways of life, which encouraged dirtiness and unkempt appearance. However, these changes were not affected during these years, but had taken place many years before.

What had always offended the other religious orders was that the Templars and other military orders had invented the status of soldier-monk, according to which they were able to draw weapons against religious enemies. For some theologians this signified an aberration of the evangelical message. The fact that their activities were commanded by the Pope had not doused the flame of disapproval and even hate.

The gravest factor was the three relentless rivals of the Temple: the hyena called Philippe IV; the jackal, Guillerme of Nogaret; and the vulture, Guillerme of Paris. The three were achieving an excellently performed job, and they would continue to do so unless stopped by a definitive sentence.

Chapter XVI

THE FARCE IS IMPOSSIBLE
TO UNRAVEL

Even though the truth came out

When Pope Clemente discovered the scandalous situation, he ordered an investigation of the proceedings, which were turning up results that were so favourable to the king and his followers. The investigation was undertaken by French cardinals, who owed their positions to the king. Thus the Pope decided to deprive the Temple of all its riches and of its religious authority.

However, in the two years that followed, so many protests were raised that Clemente V had to name a commission of clergymen to hear the Templars who wanted to defend their Order. The trial was due to start on 12th November, 1309, in Paris. This was seen as a further triumph for the king, as he had refused to allow the commission to travel around France hearing the words of the accused prisoners. For this reason he claimed that most of the heretics were in the capital, and that it was easier to bring the rest to have them all together. This reasoning would be logical if it had not come from such a manipulative man and his adviser.

The commission took several weeks to start its work, as some of its members were forced to be absent due to problems with their dioceses, sickness and other causes. There were indeed too many of these excuses of absence not to raise suspicions that some force was at work in the shadows to manipulate the situation.

One of the first to take the stand was Ponsard of Gisi, who had been the Major General of the Temple of Lyon. His testimony can be summarised by the following:

"When he was interrogated about the alleged torture he had been subjected to, he said that some three months prior to making his confession before the lord bishop of Paris, he had been taken to a dungeon, where his hands were tied behind his back so tightly that blood reached his fingertips. He was in a very small place, and he declared that if he were to be subjected to such torture he would deny everything that he had previously defended and tell them what they wanted to hear. He had gone to the place determined to bear the pain, for as long as it remained brief – decapitation, death at the stake or scalding; but that he was unable to bear prolonged torture, such as he was suffering after being imprisoned for over a year on rancid bread and water."

Another example is given in the interrogation of several Templars, who had been imprisoned in the house of God of the diocese of Elne, in Rosellon. The document is dated 1310.

As far as some of the heresies of the Temple were concerned (retractions and the act of spitting on the cross), here we can see the response of brother Raimundo Guardia, ex-commander of the house of God:

Question: "Despite the Order being constituted and holy, and approved by the Pope, were each of its members, on arrival or shortly after, forced by the host brothers to deny Jesus Christ and on occasions the cross, the Virgin Mary and all the holy saints?"

Answer: "Each of the sins that you say are terrible, scandalous and satanic."

Question: "Is it true that they told you that Christ was not God, but a false prophet?"

Answer: "We were taught that we could only achieve salvation through Jesus Christ our lord, who is the redeemer of all good Christians, and who was crucified for the good of humanity and the absolution of our sins, for his lips never uttered a bad word or a lie."

Question: "Do you dare to deny that you were forced to spit on the cross and even, on some occasions, tread it underfoot?"

Answer: "Never! We were shown the cross so that we would respect and worship it, for it represents the fullest example of how Christ suffered and gave his life for the faithful Christians. That is why every Templar has a red cross sewn on his robe, in memory of our saviour's blood spilt on the wooden cross that took his life. I will add more: on Good Friday the Templars are obliged to prostrate before the cross unarmed and barefooted with nothing on the head. We did this with devotion, and believed in the nobility of this ritual. All the brothers also did it every year on the two festivals of the Holy Cross in May and September, reciting, "We are here to worship you, our lord, and bless you. On the holy cross you redeemed the world". Only on these two festivals of the year were we obliged to go barefoot."

Brother Juan of Coma added, in his confession to the same court, a specific account of how the Temple defended the cross. They respected it so much, and loved it with such untarnished sincerity, that when they had to go to the bathroom they removed their embroidered habits so as not to dirty them.

With regard to the practice of sodomy, brother Raimundo of Guardia replied angrily, fighting to control his words:

"The rules of our order are very clear on that sin! Any brother who acted against nature would be immediately deprived of his robes, his feet shackled, his hands cuffed and chained by the neck, and then he would be thrown forever into a cell, and given only bread of punishment and water of repent for the rest of his life."

In answer to the matter of the idols that the brothers supposedly carried next to their skin, brother Bartolome of the tower, who had been chaplain of the Temple, replied:

Question: "Were you not obliged to carry the head of this idol tied with cords beneath your robes and next to your very skin?"

Answer: "Never. The brothers only used belts or linen cords over their robes."

Question: "What were these belts for?"

Answer: "I suppose they wear them for the same reason as I wear my sash, because it forms part of the attire. What is more, I have worn the sash since I entered the Temple, as the order recommends. Each of my brothers wears it day and night, but not tied to any of these idols that you mention."

Brother Bartolome of the Tower resolved the matter of the confessions in the following way:

Question: "Do you not know that all members of the religion are prohibited from confessing to anyone who is not a brother of the same order?"

Answer: "I will tell you what I have witnessed. When any brother wanted to confess his sins he would go to the order chaplain, for that was what the rules established. If the chaplain was unavailable, he was authorised to go to the Minor Brothers, who were the preachers, or in an extreme case, to a secular priest of the diocese. For all the brothers who entered the Temple, the most important thing was the strictest reverence of the good customs of the Order, of the present and of the future, and to reject any bad custom."

Many other retractions accompanied these ones, which were formed with reflection and not with fear. The removal of the threat of torture, improved prison conditions, and the fact that it was known that none of the accused had been able to make contact with each other began to turn the people in their favour.

However, Philippe IV could not permit this favour, and he called on his many resources to organise the Council of Sens as quickly as possible, in order to canonically liquidise the Temple. He achieved this in the space of only five months.

The innocent are burned at the stake

The Council started their work in April, 1310, but on the following day they received the king's order to take the fifty-four Templars who had confessed to the most serious heretic crimes and burn them at the stake.

150

Both the religious and laymen involved in the pantomime obeyed their lord's order without further hesitation. And several days later, in the grounds of the convent of Saint Antoine, the innocent men were taken to a death made more inhuman by the fact that they were burned over bonfires of specially chosen slow-burning wood. Witnesses to the events recorded that the victims died with screams of innocence, shouting the injustices subjected on the Order and giving their souls to God.

As these events were soon common knowledge, it is no surprise that the first witness taken to the trial threw himself on his knees before the court in panic and shouted:

"I cannot bear another bitter moment of this! Tell me what I am accused of, my lords, and I will confess to the death of Christ himself!"

Nobody could laugh at his declarations, though they proved clearly enough the inefficiency of revealing the truth in the court of the Inquisition. Moreover, all over France the Templars continued to be burned without waiting for sentence to be passed. Sometimes it was the bishops who signed the orders, and other times the general inquisitor Guillerme of Paris.

The new pantomime, called the Council of Vienna

The Council of Vienna began in October 1311, with the mission of deciding the future of the Temple. Philippe IV and his followers had once again returned to torture to obtain more recent testimonies of heresy. The confessions of devil worship and sodomy, and other crimes were again repeated to the courts.

The evidence soon reached the hands of the clergymen and the Pope, who was to be present at various points. The pantomime had been meticulously prepared and rehearsed, and nothing was expected to go wrong in its execution before the public. However, somebody changed the script at the last minute, for the first to take the stand not only defended the Temple, but added that between fifteen hundred and two thousand Templars were waiting around Lyon to come to their defence.

Historians have been unable to prove that this military corps existed, though it is known that a similar number of Templars had managed to escape imprisonment. Thus Clemente V and his cardinals were very scared, and immediately sent the nine accused back to prison, where the guard was tripled. But there was no attack.

The next months were taken up with negotiations, for nobody could agree on who should defend the Templars. Finally the decision was left to Clemente V, who allowed the accused men to speak. The scene took on the air of a great theatre, where the actors played the parts that had been assigned to them with no emotion, for the trials were held behind closed doors, away from the public eye.

On 6th May, 1313, the Pope dictated bulls to announce that those who had confessed their sins were to be received in the monasteries, while those who had repented of confessing to heresy were sentenced to life imprisonment. The four highest masters of the Temple were given a more severe sentence.

The death of the jackal

In this period, Guillerme of Nogaret had lost the king of France's favour, and though he was compensated with the post of royal chancellor, he no longer had access to Philippe IV's private rooms. Perhaps he had exceeded in his commitments, or perhaps the greedy king had found a preferred adviser.

The jackal died on 11th April, 1313, without having the satisfaction of seeing Jacob of Molay burned at the stake, though he had arrested him personally, and trusted that he would be present at his death. He had left everything so well prepared, without overlooking a single detail, that he must have died in the knowledge that only one result was possible: the absolute end of the Temple.

The execution of the four remaining Templars

Alejandro Vignati's words shall be used to describe the last fatal events:

"There remained nothing but for Clemente V to dictate the sentence of the four high masters of the Order of the Temple. He had been awarded the responsibility of their fate, but he was able to delegate his power amongst his most trusted cardinals, and selected those most sympathetic to his ideas. He had never been inclined to haste, and the judgment was delayed until 19th March, 1314.

"On this day, the accused were placed on a raised platform in front of Notre Dame: Jacob of Molay, the great master; Godfrey of Charney, master of Normandy; Hugo of Pernaud, inspector of France; and Godfrey of Gonneville, master of Arquitania. All had been imprisoned in the course of the last seven years, and had been told by the cardinals that they would be sentenced to life imprisonment.

"Proceedings were initiated by the pontifical delegates reading out the crimes and heresies of the Templars. Suddenly, the Knights of the Temple, the highest men of the Order, stepped forward and addressed himself directly to the people of Paris below him:

"We consider that we are guilty, but not of these crimes of which we are accused. Guilty of our own cowardice of having betrayed the Temple in order to save our own lives!"

"The words were spoken on behalf of all by Jacob of Molay, to show that all four of them had not forgotten their status as knights. None was prepared to let the Order of the Temple disappear under the mud that had been dragged over it, based on false infamy and malicious accusations formed from hatred and cruelty. They acted as though the white cape decorated with the red cross that they had been accustomed to wearing had suddenly been revealed before their eyes, like a flash of lightning. The same cape had blown in the winds of Jerusalem, in San Juan of Acre and in Cyprus, and on the highest towers of the castles and fortresses of Palestine. With all that behind them, the last Templars once again felt the glorious ghosts of the knights fallen in battle, fighting to defend their faith in the Temple; and of the dignified lords who had dedicated their lives to monk-hood, and who became martyrs in the name of their order. How could they now abandon the standard that had shined so brilliantly over so many victories and glorious defeats? The blood of man heroes had given honour to the standard that had borne the words *Non nobis, Domine, sed Nomini tuo da gloriam* (Never to us, Lord, but to your name is all glory conceded).

"So spoke the last master of the Templars, in a strong and firm voice, to the people and the cardinals Arnaldo of Saint Sabine, Nicolas of Saint Eusebius and Arnaldo of Saint Prisca, and to the king's representatives. He was not afraid to admit his weaknesses and declare the falseness of all the accusations. He took the heavens as his witness on the threshold of death, in this last gesture of medieval knighthood and suicidal passion, which at the same time was a demonstration of justice and sincerity in the name of the order that destiny had seen fit to demolish.

"The situation was completely reversed, and the accused were handed over to the cardinals. Philippe IV once again ran to his advisers. From a canonical point of view, Jacob's actions had been very significant, even causing a scandal that could not be tolerated. All Paris spoke of the event, and the authorities feared rioting.

"On that very day, at sunset, a huge pyre was laid on the small Seine island the Isle of the Jews, which was under the charge of the monks of Saint Germaine des Prés."

It is written that Philippe IV watched the events from a window. The events were witnessed and recorded by Godfrey of Paris:

"The great master removed his robes, without hesitation, as soon as he was taken to the pile of wood. I write exactly what I saw. He was left wearing nothing but his tunic. He showed great calm and no sign of fear, he was violently pushed and manhandled onto the pyre and bound to the stake in the middle. His hands were held behind his back and tied with rope, but Jacob of Molay said to his executioners: 'At least free my hands, that I may join them in prayer to God on the moment of my death. God knows that I am here as a result of great injustice, and He will take revenge for our deaths. Catastrophe will soon crash down on those who have condemned us with no respect for true justice. I die with this knowledge. To you, Lord, I beg you to look to the Virgin Mary, mother of Christ.'

"He was allowed to put his hands together, and made a

prayer that nobody could hear. Then death came to him so peacefully, and the flames could not change the expression of goodness on his face. Everybody watched in amazement. I saw some cry, and heard a murmur of protest, and I understood that a great injustice had been committed. But none had the courage to raise their voice to make their feelings known."

What happened to the executioners?

The executioners were in truth not those who took the Templars to the stake, but those who manipulated the truth and twisted the words of thousands of innocent men subjected to torture.

We know that Guillerme of Nogaret had died, and if he went anywhere it was certainly to something resembling the Christian Hell. The first of the remaining conspirators to perish was Clemente V, thirty-six days later. He had been ill, but the doctors had declared his recovery. Then one night he suddenly started to scream from an insufferable pain that gnawed his belly. The most important doctors ran to his side, but they arrived too late, only to witness the death of the Pope "at the mercy of horrible suffering."

Eight months after the death of the last Templars, the king of France fell from his horse while riding through the forest of Fontainebleau. Nobody could understand how he had not seen the branch that struck him. The blow was so strong that the king suffered general paralysis, which impeded him even from speaking. However, he was able to advertise his great suffering until the moment of his death.

The inventor of the lie, Esquieu of Floyran, ended up being stabbed to death in an alley. His attackers were never identified, in a similar fate to many of the other minor and major players in the pantomime of events.

When the people heard of these deaths, one of the most enigmatic legends of the world was born. Though the legend was based on of Jacob Molay's vengeance, the reaction of some French Temples is worth noting, for over a thousand of them could have saved his life.

It seems that a group of Templars awaited nightfall, after the people had finished scavenging in the ashes of the victims to take them home as relics. The mysterious Knights of the Temple contented themselves with the ashes of the wood, a fistful of which they threw in the direction of the king and pronounced an ancient curse, the *Machbenach*, which came from the times of Solomon and had always proved very effective.

Did the ashes and the curse assist in the vengeance sworn by the last master? The most sceptical historians put it down to a series of coincidences, though it may seem impossible that there were so many in such a short period of time.

The act of taking the ashes of the Templars, who were considered saints, home, was typical of the popular fervour of the Middle Ages. A priest, who was considered a living saint, had been put to death and the desperate hope was to employ his whole body as a relic. If we consider the relics kept in an infinite number of churches, we can form the conclusion that when a possible saint died a part of the body, particularly the hands and feet, were cut up to be given out as relics.

CHAPTER XVII

WHAT HAPPENED TO THE REST OF THE TEMPLARS?

The Templars in Spain and England

A long time before the four Temple leaders were burned at the stake, all Europe was discussing what would be done with all the properties and riches of the order. We know that those in France fell straight into the hands of the greedy king. Clemente V also tried to take control of the possessions in the entire continent, as a way of covering the costs of the Holy Land and organise a new crusade, according to the documents he sent to the European chancelleries.

One of the main problems arose in the discussions concerning who was to manage the copious funds. As nobody could come to an agreement on the issue, each king resorted to his own solution. The king of Aragon, for example, made it clear that he would keep a part for himself, and did not offer any explanation as to what he intended to do with the rest.

It has been calculated that the kings and princes of England received more than nine thousand, two hundred and fifty pounds sterling from the Temple's treasures between 1308 and 1313, which is equal to a quarter of the income of the

Templars in the country. Such a sum would have served to maintain all of London and its provinces for more than five months.

In 1312, Pope Clemente IV dictated the *Ad Providae* bull, which transferred all the property of the Temple to the Order of the Hospitallers. But this transfer was to be complicated. Certain high dignitaries, namely the Doge of Venice, expelled the Temples by force so they could take over their palaces and churches, and in some areas of Germany the army were given the task of with turning the Templars out of the properties.

In Spain things were handled differently. In 1317, the king of Valencia handed the goods of the Templars and the Hospitallers over to the new military order of Montera. The exchange worked out advantageous for the Hospitallers, for they thus became the owners of the Templar properties in Aragon and Catalonia. The kingdom of Castile could not divide out the properties there, since most of the castles, treasuries and churches had been passed from hand to hand. What the king did manage to seize was given to his own military orders.

The Templars' actions as isolated individuals or as groups are difficult to analyse on a global scale, because they all acted very differently. Bernardo of Fuentes, in Aragon, escaped from the castle where he served in 1310, when the brothers in France were experiencing the worst of the situation. He put himself at the service of the Sultan of Tunisia, in a Christian militia. His good work must have been noticed by his lord, and he was named ambassador three years later. He was to carry out this role in many European courts.

In general, according to the abundant documentation that exists, it can be confirmed that the order was loved and respected throughout Spain. As they had been witnessed fighting throughout almost two centuries in the Reconquest, their excellent military spirit, ability to manage the possessions they had earned, and the ease with which they adapted to the customs of each place was highly admired. At the time the order was abolished, most of the Templars had been born in Spain.

What happened in other European countries?

A large number of the Templars from Germany and other countries of central Europe ended up in prison, despite having changed their appearance and customs. Each one had to give up all his possessions, though there were exceptions, for some of the judges were able to see the Templars' innocence, interpret the laws according to the situation, and set them free. They also received a pension as compensation for all the confiscated possessions. In Toulouse the knights were awarded a pension of eighteen coins a day and the sergeants nine. These sums allowed the beneficiaries to live the lives of rich bourgeoisie, though most of them used their money to help their less fortunate brothers in prison. Their families were also attended to, for one of the principal qualities learned in the Order was that of solidarity with brothers in need.

What happened in Italy and those in France?

The Templars in Italy, as almost everywhere, were considered innocent of the charges dictated by the papal documents, although certain precautions were taken. In Ravenna, the members of the Temple had to undergo a sort of religious purging before the bishop, which consisted of swearing in front of seven witnesses, well-known to them, that they had not committed heresy and that they were prepared to respect all civil and religious laws and maintain an honourable life.

Amongst the many legends that extended through Europe at the time, it was told that the Templars were necromancers, alchemists and that they organised celebrations of witchcraft. It is possible that some Templars were involved in such practices, and spread the idea that all the members of the order did the same in secret places. The people would never forget all the barbarities exposed during the long trials held in France and other countries, which never questioned the existence of satanic rituals and the worship of Baphomet, and other practices of witchcraft and black magic.

The Order of the Hospitallers was charged with providing regular income for the large number of Templars who were found innocent, as they had taken over the treasures of the Temple. But several ex-Templars married, against the rules of celibacy of their old Order, and the new Pope had to dictate bulls in reference to the matter of pensions, which reduced the total sum by only a little.

In French Roussillon, a few Templars were able to continue to benefit from their possessions, having been declared innocent of the accusations presented by Philippe IV. But these few were the exception, for many more were still dying in the prisons, despite the repeated public clamours for their freedom. The demands were ignored while the inquisitors and guards who had affected the arrests and charges were still alive, for they were not prepared to recognise that they had committed an error of such proportions.

Chapter XVIII

THE HEIRS OF THE TEMPLARS

The revival of the Templars

It is known that during the reign of Louis XIV a society called the Resurgence of the Templars existed, which included some of the country's most important noblemen, such as the Duke of Gramont and the Marques of Biran. With the outbreak of the French revolution, the name was changed to Bull Head. Its master was the Duke of Cosse-Brissac, who handed over command to the doctor Ledru when he was taken prisoner. Ledru took charge of the revival of the Order, and joined forces with the Mason Frabré-Palaprat.

They needed to give their Order more authenticity, and so began the search for objects that had belonged to members of the Temple. It is told that an antiquarian gave them the sword, mitre and helmet belonging to Jacob of Molay, and that they were also able to exhume the bones of the last master of the Temple, for which they had to go to the place where he had been burned at the stake, and there they found the grave.

One of the conditions imposed on all those who wished

to enter the new order was that of pure blood – members that had been born into nobility. This went strongly against the ideals of the revolution, and the order was thus forced to become clandestine. However, during the Napoleonic years they achieved great importance with his support.

Alejandro Vignati writes the following in *The Enigma of the Templars:*

"The new Order of the Templars took care to establish particular rites and initiation ceremonies. The lodges were called encampments, and its officials attempted to recreate the attire and personal appearance of the original Templars. The distinctive characteristics, a beard and a sword, were supplemented with several passwords and secret signs of communication. These were made up of phrases, handshakes and other diverse signals, which were modified according to the different encampments. The members were given the name of 'lord knights' and all wore habits and carried poisoned swords. Any man who wished to be initiated into the Order had to present himself dressed as a pilgrim, with a coarse cloak, simple sandals, carrying a staff in his right hand and also a bag and a belt or rope around the waist. In several 'encampments' the new member had to carry a bag on his back, which he then threw to the ground to make the sign of the cross. As he approached the 'lord knight' that was to anoint him, a trumpet announced the beginning of the ceremony. A military-style talk was heard, and his forehead was touched with a sword by the second captain of the Order in the presence of representatives of all the 'lord knights'.

"When the master of ceremony asked the novice, he had to answer that he considered himself a real pilgrim, prepared to consecrate his existence for the good of the poor, sick and needy, and defend the Holy Sepulchre. After walking seven times around the encampment, and exchanging the staff for a sword, the oath was repeated, swearing to defend the sepulchre of Jesus Christ against the Jews, Turks, infidels and pagans, and in general against all the enemies of the Gospel. He would then add the words 'If I violate this oath, as a brother of the Temple, may my head be split in two by a jagged sword, my brain removed from my skull, and the two placed in separate baskets; my brain roasted under the rays of the sun, and my head immolated in honour of Saint John of Jerusalem, who was the first soldier and martyr of our Lord and Saviour; and that moreover my soul, which in life resides in my head, be presented to God the following day to be accused. May God protect me!'

"Once these words were spoken, the novice took a candle in his hand and walked five times around the 'encampment' in deep meditation. Then he would kneel to be armed as a knight by the Commander, who said, 'With this I declare you and arm you Hospitaller Mason knight.' Then the Commander draped a cloak on his shoulders, placed the smock over his head, and handed him the sword and shield. Lastly, he was indicated the holy sign of the Order, which was Mediterranean."

The Masons

The Templars left thousands of testimonies in cathedrals, churches, hermitages, towers and other buildings, which can today be found all over Europe. Spain alone has hundreds of ruins in Galicia, Catalonia, Valencia, Castile, Leon, Extremadura and other regions. Among them are gargoyles, porticos, columns, floors, walls, window panes, and other architectonic elements that demonstrate Templar figures, though they have been worn by time and the weather. The octagonal churches and hermitages are perhaps some of the most beautiful facets of the legacy.

However, these testimonies can be considered as those that are made in the tomb, which nobody will dare to open. This must have happened over the course of more than five centuries, until in the eighteenth century the Masons gathered them together. The first encampment was constituted in London. During the festival of Saint John the Baptist of 1723 the Constitutions were published, the aim being to found the new association, called Operative Masonry (association of English builders).

In perfect accordance with illuminist ideology, the Masonry quickly spread amongst the aristocratic and bourgeois classes of Western Europe and North America. It was introduced in France in 1725 by Lord Waters, and in 1801 dissident Masons founded the Scottish Rite, which soon became popular in France, Belgium, Holland and South America.

One of the factors that most contributed to the vast acceptance of the Masons can be attributed to their attire. The founders of the order chose robes that were very similar to those worn by the ancient soldier-monks, and their rites and ceremonies resembled those of the Templar Order. The new members were told on entering the encampment that Masonry had originated from a legacy that was taken to Scotland by Templar knights who had escaped from persecution in France. This legacy was that of Jacob of Molay. In one encampment, initiates were shown an old candelabrum of Hebrew craftsmanship, and told that it was from the Temple of Jerusalem.

In 1804, the Great Orient of France officially recognised the Scottish Rite, but gave it another name: Ancient and Accepted Scottish Rite. The truth is that the two Rites differed in no more than the occasional symbol of external ceremony.

In eighteenth century Spain, some members of the Masonry, such as the Count of Aranda, Campomanes, Jovellanos, Riego, Espronceda, Espartero and many others held important positions in society and politics. We know that in the twentieth century Francisco Franco, before being named *Caudillo* of Spain, wanted to join the Masons, but was not admitted.

With the group's swell in popularity, new rituals continued to be incorporated, such as the one in which members had to curse the memory of the three great enemies of the Templars: Pope Clemente V, King Philippe IV and the Templar knight who started the fatal rumour, who was given the name Noffodei.

The Count Saint Germain

The Masons adopted the abolition of the French monarchy as their principal objective, as they represented one of the three great enemies. For this reason they were found among the revolutionaries that condemned Louis XVI and Marie Antoinette to the guillotine.

The Gnostic sect of Saint Jakin was also formed in the eighteenth century, and from the very beginning was centred on magic and the secrets of the Rosenkreuz – similar in many ways to the Masons – and the Templars. This peculiar name was chosen from the names inscribed in the most important columns of the Temple of Solomon: Jakins and Bohas, due to the fact that the Hebrew 'J' is the sacred *jod* of the alphabet, as it is the initial of the names Jehovah and Jahve. However, the name Jakin was used to confuse the profane and maintain profound religious communication secret.

Amongst the *sanenjakinites*, the count of Saint Germain stands out as one of the most mysterious and important people of history. His entire biography was concerned with enigmas, throughout his entire life. Some said that he was the son of a Portuguese judge, others that his father was a Rabbi, and others swore that he became a Jesuit in Spain with the surname Aymar.

What nobody doubted is that he had knowledge of the entire history of the Templars. The great lover Casanova met him several times, and wrote of the experience:

"I have never heard anybody speak with such eloquence and fascination, he reasoned in such an extraordinary way that his words were understood both by wise and ignorant men, for he addressed them on the same level. He knew all the languages of the Earth; he played many musical instruments, and knew the secrets of alchemy; he painted the portrait of a lady in just a few hours with the art of a great master; and he could make any woman he desired fall in love with him."

The count of Saint Germain was received straight away in the palace of Versailles, however he refused to make any appointments or accept any invitations. He appeared in places when he so wished, always wearing balsams, elixirs, creams and oils. He had manufactured magic water that detained the ageing process, and according to the stories told about him he lived to be two hundred.

What we do know for sure is that one afternoon he entered the palace wearing an outfit adorned with diamonds, which were valued by the expert opinion of the jewellers who saw him at over two hundred thousand pounds. When the police investigated him, it was discovered that he had no bank account, received no money from any business or client, and never used any bills to pay. So from where did he obtain such fabulous wealth?

There is no doubt that he had achieved the ultimate dream of the alchemist: the philosopher's stone, in other words that he knew the secret of changing any metal into gold, or diamond. Another legend that was attributed to the count of Saint Germain told that he built an alchemy workshop in the cellars of Versailles, where he taught Louis XV the secrets of the hermetic science. That would explain how Louis XV found the best way of overcoming the economic crisis. On one morning he arrived at the Central Bank of Paris with several chests, which contained one hundred million pounds worth of gold coins. Had he obtained them with the use of the philosopher's stone, as the representative of the Templars had taught him?

Years later, the Count of Saint Germain conspired with the Masons to overthrow of the French monarchy. It is said that the anonymous threats received by Marie Antoinette were his work, detailing how, when and where she was to die, though her death came before the date forecast, on 4th February, 1784. The Count sent a letter to the intimate friend of the queen, Madame Adhemar:

"All is lost for the French nobility, Lady Countess. The sun that shines on us today will be the last that the monarchy ever sees. Tomorrow there will be no such thing: there will be chaos, and total anarchy. You can be certain that I have tried everything to turn destiny around, but it has been impossible, and now it is too late. I cannot impede the work of this devil who calls himself Cagliostro, whom you must avoid at all cost. I will try to protect you, but be prudent. This tempest that I warn you of will not touch you. I yearn to run to your side. What could we advise each other in this situation? You would beg me to save the king and queen, and this is now out of my hands. Neither can I detain the fact that the Duke of Orléans, who will triumph tomorrow, but who will cross the capitol after a race and hurl himself from the summit of the rock Tarpeya. But if you still desire a meeting with an old friend, go to the mass at eight, in the Recoletas, in the second chapel on the right hand side.

Count of Saint Germain."

The countess kept the appointment, though she was terrified by the fate of her friends. Amongst the shadows she found the wise old alchemist, alive and untouched by any sickness. She asked him from where had he come, and the mysterious Templar heir answered from Japan and China.

As in the story, all the predictions were fulfilled, for the overthrowing of the monarchy and the death of the Duke of Orléans immediately took place. This gives the count of Saint Germain logic-defying abilities. He was further seen by people in different continents and periods, always in full health. The count also claimed to have been in the court of Cleopatra, with Hernan Cortes in Mexico, and in the second and Third Crusades as one of the knights of the Order of the Temple.

Was Cagliostro a demon?

The count of Saint Germain alerted Madame Adhemar to a demon named Cagliostro. It is not likely that he was referring to the famous person that Alejandro Vignati writes of in *The Enigma of the Templars:*

"Cagliostro has been recognised as an agent of the Temple. This is why he sent a circular to the London Masons to advise them to offer their most solid collaboration, for the time had come to rebuild the Temple of the Eternal. Like the ancient knights of the Holy Land, he practiced black magic and the mysterious science of evoking spirits. He could tell the past and present, make predictions for the future and realise prodigious healing miracles.

"He brought a new ritual to the Masons, called de *Isis*, in which he appeared with his head wrapped in strips and crowned with a small sphinx of Thebes. He liked to hold solemn night ceremonies, in rooms where the walls were covered with hieroglyphics illuminated by medieval torches. His priests chose beautiful girls, which he called 'my doves', and whom he entranced into a state of ecstasy, so they would act as oracles. For this he used hydromancy, because water is an excellent conductor, powerful reflector and a refrigerating element, particularly by starlight, and was used in a similar way to the illusions that appear in the ocean or the clouds.

"Cagliostro had become a follower of Mesmer, and thus acted as a medium, especially impressionable, neurotic, blessed with both delicacy and strength, that he used to stimulate the imagination of the girls he used. He was accustomed to carrying with him a bust of his own head, on which was inscribed 'To the divine Cagliostro'. Having achieved god-like worship from the people, the powers of justice treated him as an intriguer, a charlatan, the procurer of his own wife, and above all, a heretic. The Roman inquisition condemned him to life imprisonment, and the people of Europe were profoundly shocked. However, the outbreak of the French Revolution stole the general attention for itself, and Cagliostro was momentarily forgotten.

"But the Templar's acts offer many details of evidence of the true processes of the cabbala, for his seal deserves as much attention as Solomon's seal, as it proves that he was educated in the secrets of science. This stamp explained via cabbalistic letters, called *Acharat* and *Althotas*, shows the basic characteristics of the high secret and the great work: a serpent pierced by an arrow, on which is written the first letter alpha of the Greek alphabet, and the figure of the fusion of the active beginning with the light. The arrow belongs to Apollo, and the serpent represents Python or the green dragon of hermetic philosophy. The letter alpha signifies unity in perfect equilibrium. This pentacle is represented in different ways on the talismans of the ancient magic, with the serpent sometimes replaced by Juno's peacock, with its royal head and its tail lowered, or by a white lamb pierced through by a cross, as is seen on the shield of the French town of Rouen."

Who was Cagliostro?

Cagliostro performed prodigious cures in different places all over Europe, of which the authenticity can never be put into doubt, as the beneficiaries were Counts, Dukes and people of high social standing whom the doctors had given up on. He freed Baroness Strogonow from the grips of madness, cured the Marques of La Salle from the gangrene that was eating his legs away, and eliminated cancers that threatened the existence of other great men.

He also installed clinics in Paris, where he treated the most important people in the city from six o'clock in the morning until nine o'clock at night. But he charged them large sums for his interventions. For poorer people it was a different matter, for he prescribed them easy remedies for their complaints and did not accept a single coin for his trouble.

He also set aside a large part of his time to introducing the new rites of Isis to the masons, as it was one of his duties as representative of the Templars. Some years later he was forced to flee Paris when he was accused by Marie Antoinette of stealing her famous necklace.

He arrived in Rome in 1789 in the company of his wife. He made immediate contact with the nobles and the most important people of the city, after presenting himself in the masons' encampment, so that they would know him as one of their highest leaders. He was doing a good job that promised to bring him fame and riches, when the unexpected happened. His faithful wife, Serafina, reported him to the Holy Office as a witch and a mason. She also took the trouble to find out his real identity: he was called Guiseppe Balsamo, and he had been born in the low quarters of Naples. He had always been an adventurer, who before beginning his act as a magician had held some rather lower positions.

Cagliostro was arrested on 27th December, 1789. He was judged and condemned to life imprisonment. And in 26th August, 1795, he died in the midst of horrible convulsions in the fortress of the castle of Saint Angel.

However, legend tells a different tale. According to the

ancient story he was not condemned to life imprisonment but to death. On the very morning of his execution, the representative of the Templars asked for a priest so that he could confess. After an hour, the priest was seen to leave the castle, but later, when the guards entered the cell, they found the real priest lying on the floor, dead and semi naked. The prison doctor was called, and he verified the cause of death as strangulation. Nobody knew where Cagliostro was to be found, nor where he might have gone. Though as often happens in these cases, many people swore they had seen him in many different places. We have to remember that like the count of Saint Germain, Cagliostro had confessed that he was immortal.

The doctrine of the great Copto

Alejandro Vignati informs us of the meaning of this doctrine:

"The title that Cagliostro had assigned to his teachings was that of the Doctrine of the great Copto. As can be seen on their study, they presented the double function of regenerating the physical and moral faculties of human beings. The imposed rules of the Great Copto to obtain the first of these faculties were the following:

"Climb the Sinai at the hand of Moses, the Calvario and the Tabor with Phales and the Carmelo with the prophet Elias. On the highest part of the mountain you must build your tabernacle. It will consist of three houses, and the one in the centre must be three storeys high. The middle storey will hold a round room, with a dozen beds placed around the walls and another in the centre; reserved for sleep and dreams. The highest floor, which will be the third storey, you will build square and you will put sixteen windows, four in each wall, for this will be the floor of light. There you will pray alone, for a period of forty hours, and you will sleep the same number of nights in the bedroom of the twelve masters. If you fulfil these precepts, you will obtain the knowledge of the seven geniuses, and then they will give you the pentagram that is

170

drawn on the sheet of virgin parchment: this represents the hidden character of the white fox that is told in the prophecy of the smallest of the twelve masters. Your spirit will at that moment be illuminated by the divine fire, and your entire body will acquire the purity of the most innocent child. Your capacity of penetration will go beyond all limits, tiredness and journeys, though they may be long and hard. Your power will reach new almost infinite bounds, and you will start to enjoy the perfect position of rest, which is the first sign of immortality. You will be able to shout with joy and full merit: 'I have managed to become the person I am!' Nothing and nobody will pass you, nor age or illness wound you."

Having read the doctrine of the great Capto there is no doubt that Cagliostro knew the Cabala perfectly, for the three places consisted of the union between the physical human with his religious yearning and his philosophical mind. The dozen masters that are mentioned must be seen as the revealers.

To obtain the great secret of physical regeneration the mysterious rules of Copto must be followed:

"To celebrate every fifty years a forty-day rite, like a type of jubilee, but so that it falls on the full moon of the month of May. Moreover, the chosen places must be in the country, and he must be accompanied by only one person, the most loyal. The chosen one must fast throughout this whole time and drink nothing more than the spring dew that he may collect from the wheat with a silk cloth or a canvass of white thread. If the hunger becomes too strong, he may eat some tender shoots. He will begin the meal with a large goblet full of dew, and finish with a single sponge or a crust of bread. On the seventeenth day he must perform a slight bleeding, but with the precaution of drinking six drops of balsam in the morning and six drops in the afternoon. The quantity will be increased over the following days, until he reaches thirty-two drops. After this period, on the following morning he will repeat the bleeding, being careful to spill only a small quantity of blood. Then the chosen one may lie down on the bad, where he will remain until the end of the forty days. On the instant that he awakes he will drink a vial of universal medicine. This will cause great lethargy, even fainting, that will last only three hours, and he will then suffer great convulsions, sweating and vomiting, which will oblige him to change his clothes and the bed sheets. He must immediately drink a bowl of oxen soup, with no fat, seasoned with rue, valerian, vervain and lemon balm. The following morning he will drink another vial of universal medicine, which is astral mercury mixed with gold sulphur. And after another day he will bathe in warm water.

On the thirty-sixth day he will drink a glass of Egyptian wine; on the thirty-seventh another vial of universal medicine. This will bring deep sleep. The chosen one will soon say that they were changing his hair, his teeth and his nails, and his skin. On the thirty-eighth day he will bathe in the aromatic herbs already mentioned. On the thirty-ninth he will take two spoonfuls of red wine and ten drops of elixir of Acarat. On the fortieth day, the great task will be completed, and the old man will see that he is completely rejuvenated."

As we can see, the great Copto was taken from the Cabala, which he perfected to achieve immortality. Cagliostro swore that he was immortal, as did the count of Saint Germain. Can we believe them?

The most honest solution is to leave the evidence unturned, and later allow each person to decide according to knowledge and principles. Yet the enigma will always remain.

The Templars in the nineteenth century

At the beginning of the nineteenth century, the Templars stopped being a primordial objective for romantics and were converted into martyrs of freedom and symbols of human injustice. Historians such as Gabriele Rossetti, Hammer and others presented the Middle Ages as a great front, during which raged a unique battle between two powerful forces: the established Church, ambitious and repressive, and the dummy powers, which included the Templars, the Catharists, the Albigenses, the knights of the Grail and all the other heretics.

For the Templars, their high purpose was to implant a new society, controlled by a group of initiated knights, who would have enough knowledge, mostly obtained through the Cabala and alchemy, to implant a justice capable of redeeming humanity. This would then be able to balance out the share of world produce equally amongst everybody, and eradicate hatred, evil and greed. But the labour toward this utopia was not a pacific task, for first they must exterminate all the heretic reactionaries – the Church.

So are we to think that the Templars were prepared to do this from inside? As infiltrators, taking the habits and conventions of the enemy, they made the most of all the advantages offered them, to plan the definitive attack.

This brings us to an issue that many nobles who fought in the crusades of the Holy Land had confronted. When they realised the power and strength of the Temple, it occurred to them that had the Templars proposed the idea, they could have erased the Muslims from the Holy Land in very little time.

So why was the idea never proposed? Perhaps because they needed to gain time in order to undermine the enemy before making the final sweep? There is no doubt that they were more in tune with the innovations or the era than any other social or religious group. They were the first to open a bank, which was the base of the idea that has perpetuated until today; to support gothic art, which they used in their splendid cathedrals; the first to administrate with such efficiency their multitude of property; and to embrace the techniques of the infidels in peace as in wartime. The structure of the Muslim sect of assassins under the 'Old Man of the Mountain', and the Order of the Temple was the same. They offered identical services to the devout who worshipped and shared interests such as consuming hashish and enjoying bisexual carnal relations, although understood as a form of knowledge and not as a vice.

173

The theories of Eliphas Levi

Halfway through the nineteenth century, the Frenchman Alphonse-Louis Constante, known as Eliphas Levi, dedicated a number of books to the subject of the Templars. His vision was a very peculiar one that transferred the soldier-monks to the Egypt of Osiris and to Palestine, where Jesus and John the Apostle walked together. According to Eliphas Levi, the Order of the Temple had intended to end papal dominion, and so recurred to Baphomet. Rather than a demon, Baphomet represented a compendium of the philosopher's stone, the Cabala and the God of absolute science. Thanks to his intervention they would achieve a world ruled by harmony, solidarity and goodness, once having eliminated all the opposing forces.

This aim of course was totally anti-clerical, as were the aims of the masons, and was supported by a large number of intellectuals. Great con-men and fraudsters, such as the English magician Alistair Crowley became involved, who found a message of sexual magic in the Templar Order that began with the arrival of the initiated, obliged to consent to sodomy in return for the right to join the Order.

The nostalgia of the Temple

During the twentieth century, several different associations were established, each claiming to be the authentic successors to the Temple Order. In 1990 one of them, called *Ordo Supremus Militari Templi Hierosolymitani*, organised a congress in the Portuguese city of Faro, attended by so many representatives from countries around the world, all prepared to recover the best of the Templars, that they ended up writing to the Vatican to urge the Pope to recognise the 'historical error', when Clemente V consented to the destruction of the Temple.

However, the masons and the Rosenkreuz are those who best represent the Templars, at least according to their rituals and attire. In more recent times a secret sect has appeared, called Priory of Sion, that sees itself as the Templars' direct successors, but from a different concept: that of the Christian religion seen from an esoteric point of view, which preaches the creation of a family from the union between a descendent of Jesus and Mary Magdalene and the heir of a ancient French noble family.

Years ago in the United Kingdom a Bedouin encampment was set up, based in Bristol, and in which many of the Temple customs are maintained. They have encampments in other cities in Britain and North America, and one of the most interesting points is related to the end of the principal initiation ceremony. One of the knights, dressed in a chef's apron and hat and with a huge butcher's knife, approaches the new member and says, "Sir Knight, I challenge you to be just and noble in your respect of the Rules of the Order. Should you behave to the contrary, I, as a cook, will cut the spurs from your ankles with this knife."

This was an interesting interpretation of the ancient Temple rules, and one which gives the impression of triviality. On the other hand, what does demand respect is a western sector with such enthusiasm for Templar literature, including that which refers to its history, its mysteries and its enigmas. There are thousands of books and documents available for consultation on the subject, though it is important not to be overwhelmed by the process, for the human drama, the complexity of the relations with the Holy Land and the entire extraordinary world of the Middle Ages is fascinating. For this reason it is always advisable to seek the help of somebody who is knowledgeable on related topics, and study the events with the widest scope possible.

CHAPTER XIX

THE TEMPLARS AND
THE GREAT MYTHS

Did the Templars reach America?

Fulcanelli, author of the wonderful twentieth century work *The Mystery of Cathedrals*, and who also wrote under the name Louis Charpentier (from whom we have quoted numerous times in this book), considers it possible that the Templars reached America. He presents endless clear evidence of the fact.

One of his main reasons is that the Templars had their own fleet, ports on both the Mediterranean and the Atlantic, and they knew, long before Christopher Columbus, that the world was round. The departure of a voyage to the New World would have been from Portugal, where Columbus arrived to look for finances for his journey and to study the maritime maps that were kept in its universities, which were considered the most complete in the world.

Historian Juan de Varende wrote in *The Gentlemen* that the Templars travelled to and from America in ships laden with silver. But these ships set off neither from Portugal

177

nor England, but from the Nordic countries. The tale is not based on fantasy, and it doesn't call into question Columbus' discovery or the patronage of Spain, although it does claim that the Vikings arrived in North America and established support bases, though not colonies. During the eleventh and twelfth centuries the climatic situation was very favourable for these voyages. The warm sea meant that no icebergs were present in the North Pole, and the Viking ships were able to sail west to the coasts of Greenland and Canada. Why could the Templars not have done the same?

We know now that the Portuguese navy of the twelfth century was prohibited from sailing beyond Cape Mogador without flying the Templar flag. Vasco de Gama commanded a fleet belonging to the reformed Templars when he discovered India, a fact which can only extend the idea of the maritime knowledge of the Temple.

In pre-Columbus America a legend existed, formed in Yucatan, that told of white-skinned men arrived on the coasts in great ships, which shined like gold and slipped through the waves like enormous serpents. The men that came off the ships were tall, attractive and blue-eyed, and wore strange clothing. On their foreheads they bore a symbol of two entwined serpents, and they were given the name *chanes*. They were so generous that they searched for the wise men of the Mayas to communicate their great knowledge.

Several other similar legends can be found in Mexico and the Caribbean. One of the facts that most surprised the religious men who travelled with Columbus was that the natives were not alarmed to see either the cross or the armed knights. It has been suggested that they were even expecting them, in accordance with traditions that spoke of "one day great men will come from the sea, dressed in metal, who will bring positive changes to our lives." We know that Hernan Cortes was greeted by great support from the natives due to these beliefs.

Further solid evidence presented by Louis Charpentier referred to silver. In those times there were very few mines in Europe, Asia and Africa, considering the enormous quantities that existed in the high Middle Ages, so much that coins were minted. If we accept that it would have been impossible for the mines existing in the territories known until the fourteenth century, when the Templars were exterminated, we must acknowledge that a large part of the silver must have been transported from America in the ships of the Templars. The voyages must have been frequent, until the time when the soldier-monks officially ceased their existence.

Were the Templars alchemists?

Another possible source of such huge amounts of silver could be attributed to the Templars' knowledge of the philosopher's stone, which not only changed non-noble metals into gold, but also helped to achieve other noble metals such as silver. The count of Saint Germain, who admitted to being an heir of the Templars, proposed an alchemy workshop to the king of France, and it has been claimed that the high quantity of diamonds that adorned his clothing were obtained from alchemy. Perhaps he found the way to change normal coal into diamonds.

From a non-fanatic, sceptical study of alchemy, we know that many of the great masters achieved the trophy of the philosopher's stone and other conquests, always in isolated circumstances, with great patience and demonstrating exceptional devotion to the process. The task had many religious facets, because they were monks of science, who were respected and not feared. As they were aware of the risks involved in mixing certain materials and liquid components in new experiments, they took great precautions. We have already made it clear that the Templars were exceptional people, who were the first to reveal the great secrets of humanity. For that reason, considering the limitations of the people that surrounded them, they served as the symbol, the secret message and the communication between equals, that could be maintained even in the presence of others. Louis Pauwels and Jacques Bergier explain this type of communication in

The Return of the Sorcerers: the superior beings had no need of a foreign language, nor to create a new tongue amongst themselves, they could use the same one to communicate with each other that they used with everybody else.

Is it possible that the Temple leaders, like Jacob of Molay, were so submissive faced with their extinction because they knew that another life existed, which was very different to that described in the Bible and the Gospels?

Reincarnation

The count of Saint Germain claimed to have achieved it, and the occurrence with the Countess offers testimony: before dying he sent her an invitation, the time and place of which must have been after the doctors had declared him dead. He appeared in church with no signs of illness, and when the countess asked him where he had come from, he answered from China and Japan. Perhaps in addition to the gift of reincarnation he was able to mentally and physically divide, to travel by whim to far-off places and exist in two places at once.

There is a theory described by a science fiction author, in a novel that I read a long time ago (I regret that I have forgotten the names of both), that claims that by knowing exactly the place to which one desires to travel, with its geographical co-ordinates, by use of great mental effort it is possible to reach that place instantly, more swiftly than passing through a door, and with no regard for the thousands of miles that may lie between.

Many religions believe in reincarnation, particularly in the Orient. Some believe that we must pass through the forms of all animals in creation, in a lengthy pilgrimage that ends with an omnipotent knowledge, while others speak of reincarnation with no memory of the past, and that we all die to be reborn, with no recollection of past presence.

Parapsychological experiments have demonstrated,

beyond any doubt, that some people have been able to remember places, events and people from other eras, often after recovering from an accident or a serious illness. The German nurse Helda Bauer healed a patient who was on the brink of death after a car crash, and later remembered the city of Florence, where she had never been, and started to talk Italian, and describe people, events and places with such surprising accuracy that she went to the city. Helda was disconcerted to find herself in a familiar place, where she had never been. She remembered old locations, and took her companions to places in which she had never set foot. She spoke of people who had lived eighty years before, and it was finally deduced from the information she provided that in her previous existence she had been an Italian called Anna Zavatini, who died in 1924.

Thus maybe it is possible that Jacob of Molay was reborn into a new body. He lived without ever having to recount his new life, and later helped those who wanted to revive the Order of the Temple to find his bones, sword and robes. In this terrain of enigmas, why put the brakes on our imagination?

Immortality

Cagliostro taught us how to achieve immortality with his Great Copto. There is no evidence that anybody performed the ritual, as some of the elements necessary were only known to the heir of the Templars. But does an immortal really need to go around bragging about it just to nourish their own vanity?

If eternal life is combined with eternal youth, what are the problems that a person would face living in a normal world? Pragmatically, we could say administrative and social problems, such as identity documents, registering with the health authorities and relationships with other people, who would be bound to notice the lack of the ageing process. To resolve these problems, the immortal would have to remain only a short time in each place, moving between cities and countries, and changing identity.

Supposing that there were many immortal Templars, would they not have had unimaginable resources to defend themselves from the suspicion of the outside world? In the world, when an extraordinary event occurs it is normally divulged by means of communication. We are very used to people telling of their supernatural experiences on television, some of whom publish articles or books. But it is easy to understand how maintaining silence is the best way to allow the extraordinary to develop in peace.

The Templar symbols

Historians of the Temple Order, such as Alejandro Vignati or Juan García Atienza, have traced giant geometric forms and letters over the land of France and Spain, into which different Templar buildings fit perfectly, as though they were constructed to form a gigantic symbol, something like the constellations made by the stars.

The ancient civilisations gave the constellations the names of mythical animals and Gods. The constellation of Gemini, one of the favourite of the Templars, is situated above the French town of l'Aigle, and Orion is over Razés, in the region of Renne, and which was on the route of the Celts to the ancient menhirs.

The goat is in the sky over Paris, and the ram follows the chariot, as the eagle was able to advance over the heavens towards the horizon, to be crowned once again by the golden dawn sun in Capricorn. Exactly at the end of this astral sign was where the leaders of the Temple were burned at the stake, so they may remain in that place until the birth of the next eagle.

But the Templars not only looked toward the sky. Many of their symbols are demonic or obscene, as seen in many of the Temples, abbeys and cathedrals that they built. Those who have dared to search in the dark corners for secrets hidden amongst the shadows have found demons resembling Baphomet, with peasants performing acts of sodomy and others, which must have been seen by religious men, but not ordered to be removed or covered. Gargoyles in the form of nightmarish monsters, over monuments that represent highest spirituality are another example. Perhaps this was a way for the Templars to poke fun at the established authorities, in the same way that carnival festivals were permitted, to allow the people to shake off their tensions, at least once a year.

It is possible, though doubtful, that the people did not recognise these profane representations. In *The Secret Purpose of the Templars*, Juan García Atienza writes:

"The Templars were the catalysers of this great total that could have been an anarchic art and that in actual fact constituted the basic unity of medieval knowledge. According to the general hypothesis, the friars of the Temple acquired in the Orient the basic principles that rule the magic structure of construction, and the custom – taken from the Islamic brotherhoods of constructors – of joining all those who would intervene in the great work in a common purpose. Initiated in the secrets of knowledge and in its expression through the language of stone, the stonemasons and constructors had acquired their skill, or at least a substantial part of it, in the Templar convents. And they had come from them framed by loggias and full of a common expressive aspiration: the desire to share the corporate results of this knowledge with the people, and thus elevate them, through this contact with the magical labour, to a specific level in the heights of universal knowledge."

Atienza is referring to the cathedrals, in which the Templars had managed to unite professional skill with love of a labour well done. Just as their glaziers obtained wonders, with materials that took centuries to copy, it is possible that their stonemasons employed some method to dissimulate the true intention of the work until it was finished, by which time it was so high or concealed in the shadows that it had to be tolerated. Could it be that as far as the obscene sculptures are concerned, there existed an accord between the supervising monk and the artist who carved them? If they were to be put in places that the human eye would not see, what did it matter if they appeared, rather than an insult, true heresy?

Absolute power

With the presentation of some of the secret societies that try to imitate the Templars, we have touched on their possible ambition of conquering the world. We have also mentioned this subject in other areas. However, here we propose another question, more closely linked to reality. The dream of the Temple was to achieve fraternal world of solidarity, in which the three great religions and predominant cultures of the western world: the Hebrew, Muslim and Christian, live side by side. Why did they not achieve this dream in their time of great strength?

It is a difficult question, if we restrict ourselves to hard facts. A few years after their arrival in Palestine, they had the opportunity to govern in Jerusalem, but they chose to help the heir of Balduino III. Something similar happened in Portugal, when the country found itself facing the dilemma of living with no government, as the people were divided into small feudal authorities, or impose a king. Once again the Templars preferred not to become involved, just as they did in countless crucial moments in the Holy Land, despite the fact that they were later forced to act.

With the riches they took to France, and those stored in their banks, they would have been able to overthrow Philippe V, and as we know, the opposite occurred. Were they not prepared?

Interestingly, with the departure of the Order of the Temple, the flourishing Islam of the great Sultans, which had respected the culture of the conquered peoples (this is how we know of the ancient Greeks and other cultures), entered a slow decline that has lasted until modern times. Currently they are a powerful nation, thanks to oil, which they consider a gift from Allah, yet their culture and splendour can in no way be compared to their previous situation.

In the West also, with the Templars' annihilation, the cultural advance appeared to cease for a period of some two hundred years, until the Renaissance and Protestantism managed to revive the march of civilisation. A civilisation that ignored the history of the Templars until long afterwards.

This is another of the doubts that humanity has concerning the soldier-monks, whose existence is cloaked in enigma, some of which we hope to have explained in this book.

BIBLIOGRAPHY

Atienza, Juan García. *The Secret Purpose of the Templars*
Barber, Malcolm. *The Templars*
Bastius, Joaquín A. *The History of the Templars*
Bergier, Jacques and Pauwels, Louis. *The Return of the Sorcerers*
Bordonove, Georges. *Everyday Life of the Templars in the Eighteenth Century*
Charpentier, Louis. *The Mystery of the Templars*
Demurger, Alain. *The Rise and Fall of the Templars*
Dumas, Alejandro. *The Temple Knights*
Eslava Galán, Juan. *The Templars and other Medieval Enigmas*
Florentin, Manuel. *The Death of the Templars*
Fulcanelli. *The Mystery of Cathedrals*
Gérin-Ricard, L. *History of the Occult*
López Santiago. *The History and Tragedy of the Templars*
Maalouf, Amin. *The Crusades as Seen by the Arabs*
Melville, Marion. *The Secret Life of the Templars*
Michalet, Julio. *The Temple, Order of the Initiation of the Middle Ages*
Ollivier, Alberto. *The Life of the Templars*
Partner, Peter. *The Murder of the Sorcerers. The Templars and their Myth*
Runciman, Steven. *The History of the Crusades*

Sánchez, Dragó, Fernando. *Gargoris and Habidis. A Magical History of Spain*
Vignati, Alejandro. *The Enigma of the Templars*
Walker, Martin. *The History of the Templars*
Planeta Publishers, Spain. *Reports of History*

INDEX